WHAT HAPPENS IN HOLY COMMUNION?

What Happens in Holy Communion?

Michael Welker

Translated by
John F. Hoffmeyer

William B. Eerdmans Publishing Company
Grand Rapids, Michigan / Cambridge, U.K.

Published jointly 2000 in the United States of America by
Wm. B. Eerdmans Publishing Company
255 Jefferson Ave. S.E., Grand Rapids, Michigan 49503
and in Great Britain by
Society for Promoting Christian Knowledge
Holy Trinity Church
Marylebone Road
London NW1 4DU

Printed in the United States of America

05 04 03 02 01 00 7 6 5 4 3 2 1

Library of Congress Cataloging-in-Publication Data

Welker, Michael.
What happens in holy communion? : Michael Welker.
p. cm.
Includes bibliographical references and index.
ISBN 0-8028-4602-5 (pbk.: alk. paper)
1. Lord's Supper. I. Title.
BV825.2.W45 2000
234'.163 — dc21
00-023128

British Library Cataloguing-in-Publication Data

A catalogue record for this book is available from
the British Library

SPCK ISBN 0-281-05291-3

Contents

INTRODUCTION

What Happens in Holy Communion?

A High Point of Christian Life — or "a Sad Colloquy" (Kant)?

Holy Communion: Seen from the Outside

What happens in holy communion? A strange question! What do you think? — People sit or stand next to each other, normally in a space for worship. They pray and they sing. Then words passed down from long ago are spoken, including words from the Bible. Usually they are spoken by the pastor or priest. The words of the Bible that appear in every celebration of the Supper are more or less the following:

> In the night in which he was handed over, Jesus, the Lord, took bread. He spoke the prayer of thanksgiving, broke the bread, and said: This is my body, given for you. Do this in remembrance of me. In the same manner after the meal he took the cup and said: This cup is the new covenant in my blood, poured out for you for the forgiveness of sins. Do this, as often as you drink it, in remembrance of me.

Then each person present receives a piece of bread, and in many churches a swallow of wine or grape juice. With a word of blessing the whole thing is over. That's all that happens in holy communion!

Such an answer to the question "What happens in holy communion?" is not wrong. Rather, it briefly describes what can be observed from the outside. However, it does not say anything about the meaning of this celebration. It also does not say anything about why Christian churches attach such great significance to the Supper. It brackets out interesting and difficult spiritual and theological questions. Puzzling statements and ones that sound weird or offensive to many people today remain unclear (my body . . . given for you; my blood . . . poured out for you; forgiveness of sins . . . ; in remembrance of me).

The simple and external description also gives no response to very simple and very external questions that many people often ask. For example:

- How often should we celebrate the Supper?
- Should only one person distribute bread and wine, or should several persons participate, or even everyone present?
- Why was or is the Supper celebrated in some churches even without a gathered community?
- Why does one church give out only bread, another church bread and wine, and another church a mush made of bread and wine?
- Is it only permissible to use bread and wine, or can, for example, milk and honey, or water and apples be used?
- Why do most Christian communities never or only seldom celebrate the Supper in the form of an actual meal?
- Is it permissible or even necessary to exclude persons from the Supper under certain conditions?
- Is it permissible for children, too, to take part in the celebration of the Supper?
- Why would some churches like to celebrate the Supper in common with other churches? Why do some churches reject fellowship with other churches in the celebration of the meal? And which churches are truthful and in the right?

Therefore, although it is not false to answer the question "What happens in holy communion?" simply by recording what can be externally observed, it is inadequate and unsatisfactory.

Holy Communion: "Source and Summit of the Church's Life"?

The celebration of the Supper has various designations among the various Christian churches of the world. The Roman Catholic Church speaks of the mass, of holy communion, or of the eucharist. In recent years the name "eucharist," which means "thanksgiving," has also found increasing use in Protestant churches, especially in ecumenical conversations and documents. Otherwise they call the celebration the Lord's Supper or simply the Supper.[1] Today, however, it is not just women and feminist theologians who take offense at talk of the "Lord's" supper.[2] Orthodox churches speak of "the divine liturgy," or they use the term *synaxis,* which means "union," community gathering. And there are still a few other names for the celebration of the Supper (see especially chapter 3).

In spite of the various designations, all the Christian churches of this world are agreed that with these various terms they designate *the one celebration* whose institution is described by the apostle Paul in the following way in 1 Corinthians 11:23-26:

> 23 For I received from the Lord what I also handed on to you, that the Lord Jesus on the night when he was betrayed took a loaf of bread,
> 24 and when he had given thanks, he broke it and said, "This is my body that is for you. Do this in remembrance of me."
> 25 In the same way he took the cup also, after supper, saying, "This cup is the new covenant in my blood. Do this, as often as you drink it, in remembrance of me."
> 26 For as often as you eat this bread and drink the cup, you proclaim the Lord's death until he comes.[3]

Although all Christian churches and faith movements take this institution as their point of reference, they have developed various forms of celebration. In principle, this variety could be creative and enriching. However, it has been understood as destructive, and has led to conflicts

1. The word here, *Abendmahl,* is the word used in the title of the German original, and generally in discussing the sacrament throughout the book. It is also the typical term for the meal in German Protestantism. In this English translation of the text the most frequent rendering of *Abendmahl* is the etymologically equivalent "Supper." Since this expression is not so common in ecclesial usage in the English language, *Abendmahl* has also been rendered here as "holy communion," a term which in the American context, unlike the German one, is not confined to Roman Catholicism.

2. German: *Herrenmahl.* The German word *Herr* covers the combined ground of the English words "lord," "sir," "mister," and "gentleman."

3. All biblical quotations are taken from the New Revised Standard Version, with occasional modifications.

that have hindered or even rendered impossible a communal celebration of the meal. Both the internal life and the external credibility of the Christian churches suffer on account of these differences.

For these reasons, particularly in the last three decades, the major Christian churches and faith movements have worked out joint declarations on the meaning and significance of the Supper. Numerous "bilateral" joint declarations exist "at the global level," in which Anglicans and Lutherans, Reformed and Orthodox, Methodists and Roman Catholics, Pentecostals, Evangelicals, and other churches and ecclesial groups have arrived at shared insights concerning the Supper.[4]

These joint declarations are in fundamental agreement that the Supper is of very great, indeed extraordinary significance for the vitality, unity, and renewal of the churches. They insist on the following emphases:

- The Supper is the highest expression of the unity of the church.
- The Supper can rightly be called "source and summit of Christian life."
- The Supper can rightly be called "foundation and criterion for the renewal of the church."
- In the Supper the communion of the faithful with Christ is renewed.
- In the Supper the unity of the members of the church is renewed in the Holy Spirit.

It is not only Orthodox, Roman Catholics, and Anglicans who agree in such statements.[5] Lutherans, Reformed, Methodists, and other theologians — pastors and other church workers, academic theologians, and church leaders beyond the congregational level — have come to such conclusions.[6] In spite of the various designations for the celebration of the Supper, and in the midst of all their other differences, the larger churches

4. Concerning individual consensus texts, and concerning the way in which these texts are cited in this work, see the appendix. Eckhard Lessing, *Abendmahl*, Bensheimer Ökumenische Studienhefte 1 (Göttingen: Vandenhoeck, 1993), offers short excerpts and overviews, as well as a good theological commentary.

5. Cf., e.g., "Moscow Statement" 1976 [A-O], p. 45; "The Unity of the Church" 1979 [O-OC], p. 404; "Eucharistic Doctrine: Elucidation" 1979 [A-RC], p. 75; "Final Report" 1981 [A-RC], p. 65; "Mutual Pastoral Aid" 1984 [RC-SO].

6. See, e.g., "Dublin Report" 1976 [M-RC], p. 352; "The Presence of Christ" 1977 [R-RC], pp. 452-53, 454; "The Eucharist" 1978 [L-RC], pp. 197, 198, 201-2, 257.

are in astounding agreement concerning the institution and the profound and fundamental significance of the Supper. But this profound significance cannot simply be read off the external process of the Supper. What then happens in holy communion — above and beyond what can be externally observed?

Why is it appropriate to call holy communion "source and summit of the church's life"? Why does the Supper have the power of renewal that is ascribed to it? Why is the church's communion with Christ renewed precisely by means of the Supper? The response to such questions has consistently been and continues to be: In the Supper the risen and exalted Christ is present! All these powers and effects proceed from the presence of the risen and exalted Christ. However, the initial effect of this response is only to deepen the perplexity.

- Do we not also claim that the risen and exalted Christ is present in the church's proclamation?
- Has not Christ also assured us of his presence "where two or three are gathered in his name"?
- Has not Christ promised his presence with and in the "least of these brothers and sisters"?

What then is special about holy communion?

Since, moreover, it is difficult or even impossible to make Christ's resurrection and exaltation comprehensible to many "modern human beings," we seem only to be exchanging one obscurity for another.

Yet suppose we could make clear even to "modern and enlightened human beings" what it means to say: Here the risen and exalted Christ is present! Even then more questions immediately arise, at least for those who are familiar with details of the Supper.

- If Christ is *present* here, why are the faithful supposed to do something in the Supper "in *remembrance* of him"?
- Why, precisely in the Supper, are they supposed to "proclaim" *Christ's death?*
- Why do they wait here for his *coming?*
- What kind of strange "presence" is this — the presence of someone who has died, and yet who is also awaited and expected?
- Why is the church grounded and renewed in the process of the Supper in a way that seems to be so unclear?

It is so simple to describe the external process of the Supper's celebration. But behind that external process, and behind the assurance that the Supper has extraordinary significance for the vitality, unity, and renewal of the churches, there lies a labyrinth of questions and problems.

Dismal Personal Experiences and Good Ones

What happens in holy communion? For years this question has left me perplexed. Although I have studied theology, am an ordained theologian, and for over twenty years now have been engaged in teaching and research that has required of me intensive reflection on issues of faith, I have gone a long time without finding a satisfying answer to this question. My perplexity arose not only from the theological questions contained in the Supper, but from the form in which the meal was celebrated.

The great philosopher Immanuel Kant characterized holy communion in general, and the words about Jesus' betrayal and self-giving in particular, as "a sad colloquy."[7] Unfortunately, on many occasions his evaluation was all too convincing to me — as far as the form of the Supper was concerned. The feast of the church's unity, the celebration of the church's upbuilding, the establishment of the communion of "Christ with his own" — this frequently presented itself to me, too, as "a sad colloquy." On the basis of these experiences I readily shared the impression formulated by feminist theologians: "In our intellectualized, spiritualized, clericalized, and male-formed Christianity, there is a rite that reminds us of something forgotten, sensuous, and bodily. By contrast, the traditional observances of the Supper communicate austerity, aridity, morbid thoughts, or a Good Friday mood." Admittedly, I could share neither the abstract opposition of "intellectual/spiritual" to "sensuous/bodily," nor the sometimes over-generalized critique of the thematization of "sin" and "sacrifice." However, I certainly could share the critique of a moralized understanding of sin, and of a false conception of sacrifice (cf. especially chapters 2, 6, and 10).[8]

Holy communion as a "sad colloquy": I think back to services of holy

7. Immanuel Kant, *The Contest of the Faculties,* trans. and intro. Mary J. Gregor (Lincoln, Nebr.: University of Nebraska Press, 1992), p. 69.

8. Frauenarbeit der Evangelischen Landeskirche in Württemberg, ed., *Wir Frauen und das Herrenmahl* (Stuttgart, 1996), p. 5.

communion in Berlin in the period after World War II, in which people stood in long lines in somber big city churches to receive bread and wine. Here one could not recognize Jesus' table fellowship. The scene had more the appearance of businesses with scarce goods. Or in recent years I see before me observances of the Supper after the actual worship service. For such observances the only word that comes to me is "private mass." To my mind, festive worship services often came to a depressing end with the gathered congregation splitting up before the Supper. Many went home. But some still gathered in the chancel — for holy communion as an "appended" worship service. Even if the actual worship service had been lovely and joyful, now the dominant mood was almost always somehow depressed. Sometimes the Lord's Prayer was spoken again, and the benediction again pronounced. Had the "actual" worship service not been in order? Was an "actual" worship service only now taking place? Was this supposed to be the "highest expression of the church's unity"? Something simply had to be wrong here!

From congregations in North America which I had experienced as particularly lively and exemplary in many respects, I remember observances of the Supper in which people simply stayed seated in the pews. Like airplane passengers being served by a flight attendant, they were offered crumbs of bread and tiny plastic cups of wine. The very thing that, according to ecclesial pronouncements, was supposed to be a "high point" in the life of the church, appeared to me here as a sad "low point" in the life of an otherwise flourishing and most lively congregation. I also remember many sad situations in German and international worship services, in which Roman Catholic Christians disconcertedly declined and walked past the proffered "cup of the new covenant." Or I think of observances of the Supper for which a splendid procession of clerics and impressive liturgical singing provided preparation. But hardly anyone responded to the invitation to the meal! My impression was that the celebration of the Supper was over before it had rightly begun.

In Russia I experienced an observance of the Supper that particularly depressed me. The celebration of the Supper began with the demonstrative closing of a curtain between congregation and clergy. Evidently the congregation was not to watch — not to mention participate in — the preparation of the Supper or the feeding of the clergy. Finally the priests came out from behind the curtain with pots in hand, in which there was a mushy mixture of bread and wine, which they shoved into the mouths of the faithful by means of long spoons — as long as the supply lasted. Not:

Take and eat. Not: There is enough for everyone — however many times we must break the bread! The impression was: The feeding of children with no voice in the matter. Indeed, a bib-like cloth was held in front of them! Of course, it was a feeding only of those who came forward quickly enough.

For a long time I did not speak about such impressions. Was I not paying too much heed to my personal sentiments? Was I only being driven by subjective impressions? Was it simply a matter of questions of taste? It is well known that concerning questions of taste the disputes can be long and without result. Some observe the Supper this way, others observe it a different way! What bothers some pleases others, or in any case is familiar to them. What in one time and in one part of the world comes across as festive, pious, and joyful, in another time and another part of the world puts people off and scares people away! Is that not the ultimate conclusion of wisdom and good sense? Why couldn't I be content with this relativism?

Then there were the numerous contrary experiences, good ones, which admittedly were more along the lines of "counter-sentiments." I have experienced many celebrations of the Supper in various Christian communities, both in Germany and in other parts of the world, both in various confessions and in ecumenical worship services, which seemed to me to be anything but "a sad colloquy." Here I thought I detected something, experienced something — albeit in incipient and fragmentary ways — of the "communion of saints and the forgiveness of sins." With whatever enduring theological uncertainty, I detected something of the gathered, edified, sisterly community of Jesus Christ, strengthened on its way. "God's peace is moving throughout the world!" — "May the body of Christ preserve you unto eternal life!" At many celebrations of the Supper, such expressions did not seem to me to be pious platitudes or pie-in-the-sky religious assertions. In a manner that was still unclear, but that at moments seemed persuasive, I had the impression that when the Supper is rightly understood and rightly celebrated, it is something totally different from "a sad colloquy." Here the church of Christ is in fact built up. Here human beings experience God's vitality in peaceful, liberated, and liberating community. Here the "presence of God's Spirit" becomes available to the senses. A creative process takes place. Something happens in holy communion which is difficult to grasp, but which is of elementary importance! But what was it?

Just as for a long time I could not explain why I found some celebrations of the Supper oppressive, so I could not speak clearly about the positive experiences. What could it mean to speak of "the Supper, rightly understood and rightly celebrated," when I was not even capable of giving expression to this understanding? Naturally I knew the many classical and more recent theological discussions of the theme "sacrament and Supper," which seemed to me "somehow" to say something right and important. However, they did not answer for me the questions: What is really important and normative in the Supper? How is the Supper celebrated in accordance with its identity? Indeed, they often seemed to brush these questions aside rather than to answer them.

Gradually I could no longer tolerate the ready response that the Supper is a "mystery." More and more, this response seemed to me to be an expression of perplexity that merely covered over the problems. In addition, I found less and less satisfaction with my spontaneous insight that here Christ becomes and is present "in person." I had no response to the criticism that such assertions generated the opposite of theological clarity. Statements such as "Christ is giver and gift" did not help me attain any dependable knowledge.

Thus my positive impressions and experiences also did not bring me further forward. They did not enable me to form a clear judgment about the diverse forms of celebrating the Supper. Why did some of them strike me as "a sad colloquy," even as dissolution — as expressions of a church that was sick, devoid of orientation, or addicted to domination?[9] Why did I go out of other celebrations of the Supper and "into the daily life of the world" comforted, strengthened, and with joyful hope? Were my questions badly put? Were my expectations off the track? Was I looking at things too emotionally and subjectively? Was I being too theologically demanding? Was I approaching worship and the contents of faith with a destructive addiction to knowledge and understanding?

This situation of perplexity changed completely unexpectedly. For a lecture course in Heidelberg and for a symposium in Princeton on "Hope for the Kingdom and Responsibility for the World," I had to devote my attention anew to the resurrection of Jesus Christ. In studying the biblical texts about the resurrection, I saw for the first time — from a distance —

9. Rainer Volp, *Liturgik: Die Kunst, Gott zu feiern*, vol. 2, *Theorien und Gestaltung* (Gütersloh: Gütersloher, 1994), p. 1186, rightly says: "The symbolic action perceivable in giving and taking, eating and drinking, and praying and speaking can uncover the shining glory and the abject misery of a church."

a way to understand holy communion. Readers who do not wish to tax themselves with the description of this somewhat steep "path of approach" can skip directly to the first chapter.

The Offensive Reality of the Risen Jesus Christ as the Key to Understanding the Supper

Holy communion focuses us on the reality of the resurrected Jesus Christ and helps us perceive this reality. Of course, with this statement we seem only to have gone from the frying pan into the fire. The difficulties in understanding what is happening in the Supper are already big enough. Still bigger are the problems that many people have with the "reality" of the resurrected Jesus Christ. When we try to get to the bottom of these difficulties, we see the following:

- Over and over again in the history of Christianity, Jesus' resurrection has been grasped as mere physical revivification.
- Over and over again, people have wanted to make the readiness to understand the resurrection as physical revivification the criterion of "true faith."
- Over and over again, however, people have also criticized the practice of equating resurrection and revivification.
- Over and over again, human beings have called the resurrection into question because they understood the resurrection only as Jesus' revivification, and could not hold the latter as true.
- Over and over again, doubts about the resurrection have been brought together with Paul's statement: "If Christ has not been raised, then our proclamation has been in vain and your faith has been in vain" (1 Cor 15:14). Over and over again, people have drawn the conclusion: the resurrection as revivification is not worthy of belief — therefore Christian proclamation is empty and Christian belief is senseless!

But is it correct to equate resurrection and revivification? Do the biblical texts in fact give the impression that the risen Jesus Christ lived together with his disciples, with the women who followed him, or with other human beings in the same manner as the pre-Easter Jesus?

There are three groups of New Testament texts that hold out the promise of giving more precise insights into Jesus' resurrection: (1) the traditions concerning the empty tomb, (2) the traditions that attest the resurrection by means of luminous appearances, and (3) the traditions that connect the resurrection with appearances involving direct personal encounter.

1. The Traditions Concerning the Empty Tomb

Because the traditions concerning the empty tomb (Mk 16, Mt 28, Jn 20) have been supported from both Christian and Jewish sides — of course with different rationales — most scholars accord them a "historical basis." Of course it is also clearly recognized that these traditions — taken for themselves — do not offer a basis for attesting Jesus' resurrection. *In principle,* the traditions that say the tomb was empty — taken for themselves — admit of four different interpretations:

a. The tomb was empty because the pre-Easter Jesus in fact was physically revivified and had gone to an unknown location. This is the interpretation on which most of the critics of the resurrection concentrate.
b. The tomb was empty because the corpse was stolen and was decomposing at an unknown location — a circumstance that is so important to critics like Gerd Lüdemann: "The statement of the fact of Jesus' decomposition is for me the point of departure for all further engagement with questions revolving around his 'resurrection.'"[10]
c. The tomb was empty because an unimaginable transposition had taken place.
d. The tomb was empty because an empty gravesite was mistaken for the real gravesite — a possibility that admittedly has only been considered by a few interpreters here and there.

All variants assume that the empirically perceivable body of the pre-Easter Jesus was withdrawn at least for a while. All conceivable interpretations of the empty tomb — from the bone-dry empirical (theft of the corpse and mistaking one tomb for another) to the magical and supernat-

10. Cf. Gerd Lüdemann, "Zwischen Karfreitag und Ostern," in Hansjürgen Verweyen, ed., *Osterglaube ohne Auferstehung? Diskussion mit Gerd Lüdemann* (Freiburg: Herder, 1995), pp. 13ff., 25-26.

ural — share the presupposition that the stories of the tomb do not offer any material for medico-juridical autopsies.

The fact that the pre-Easter body was withdrawn is admittedly not a sufficient condition for belief in the resurrection. Not only almost the entire history of interpretation, but also the biblical traditions themselves are in agreement that the empty tomb alone does not awaken solid, dependable belief in the resurrection. Even the appearances of the angels and the young man at the empty tomb with the news "The Lord is risen!" do not lead to the spread of the knowledge of Jesus' resurrection.

The first biblically attested reactions to the "empty tomb" with the appearances of messengers or angels are fear and silence (Mk 16:8), the anxiety or the public rumor that the corpse has been stolen (Mt 28:11ff. and Jn 20:2), or the impression that the claim that Jesus has risen is mere "idle talk" of women (Lk 24:11).

2. The Traditions That Connect the Resurrection with Luminous Appearances

The second group of resurrection testimonies (especially those of Paul) speak of luminous appearances, and thereby exclude the conception of a merely physical revivification of the pre-Easter Jesus (Acts 9:3ff.; 1 Cor 9:1).[11]

Numerous theologians — for example, Wolfhart Pannenberg[12] — have wanted to trace all resurrection testimonies back to such luminous appearances. In this way they have sought to get around the thorny problem of the long history of confusing the resurrection with physical revivification. They have argued that the resurrection is "historical" for at least three reasons:

a. the broad temporal dispersion of the resurrection appearances;
b. the fact that the appearances remained centered in a "disciplined" manner on Jesus' resurrection, and did not slide over into an enthusiastic expectation of general resurrection, which, according to Pannen-

11. Gal 1:15-16, Phil 3:8, and 2 Cor 4:6 are also regarded as references back to the Damascus experience and to analogous appearances.

12. Cf. Wolfhart Pannenberg, *Jesus — God and Man,* trans. Lewis L. Wilkens and Duane A. Priebe (Philadelphia: Westminster, 1968), pp. 53ff. and 108ff.

berg, would have corresponded to the eschatological expectation of the time;

c. the fact that it is highly probable that the resurrection testimonies and the testimonies of the empty tomb were spread independently of one another, which, these theologians claim, demonstrates the objective status of the resurrection event.

However, the apparently elegant limitation of the resurrection appearances to luminous appearances is problematic, because these appearances alone do not explain why and how the relation to the human Jesus becomes clear in them. We should therefore start more modestly from the assumption that *among* the resurrection appearances were appearances that in no way pointed directly to an earthly-bodily person, but were related to a luminous phenomenon "from above, from heaven." It is important that, within the framework of the various resurrection testimonies, the luminous appearances in any case excluded a confusion with conceptions of physical revivification. This is not the case with the third, most complicated group of resurrection appearances.

3. The Traditions That Connect the Resurrection with Appearances Involving Personal, Bodily Encounter

The third group of texts is offensive not only for modern thought and sensibilities. At first glance these texts do in fact seem to presuppose a revivification of Jesus. Yet upon closer examination they all contradict the impression that the resurrection is nothing but a case of revivification. They place before our eyes a remarkable "corporeality" and bodily presence.[13]

On the one hand, the risen Christ enounters the "witnesses" in a sensuous way. With eyes, ears, and hands they apprehend him by sense perception. Matthew 28:9 says that the women who meet the risen Christ

13. For greater detail, cf. Michael Welker, "Resurrection and the Reign of God," in Daniel Migliore, ed., *The Princeton Seminary Bulletin,* Supplementary Issue 3: *The 1993 Frederick Neumann Symposium on the Theological Interpretation of Scripture: Hope for the Kingdom and Responsibility for the World* (Princeton, 1994), pp. 3-16. Joachim Ringleben, *Wahrhaft auferstanden: Zur Begründung der Theologie des lebendigen Gottes* (Tübingen: Mohr-Siebeck, 1998), moves in a similar direction.

touch his feet. Luke 24:30 reports that Jesus breaks bread for the disciples reclining at table. According to Luke 24:39, Jesus invites his disciples to touch his wounds. According to John 20:27, this invitation is extended to skeptical Thomas. Luke 24:41-43 is particularly pointed: "And when he had said this, he showed them his hands and his feet. While in their joy they were disbelieving and still wondering, he said to them, 'Have you anything here to eat?' They gave him a piece of broiled fish, and he took it and ate in their presence."

On the other hand, these texts say very clearly that the risen Christ is and remains an appearance. Directly alongside the emphasis on the risen Christ's presence to the senses, the texts insist that the risen Christ is an appearance. In Mark 16:12 we read: "He appeared in another form." Mark 16:14 and other texts point to the surprising and unmediated appearance of Jesus Christ among the eleven disciples reclining at table. Various texts repeatedly emphasize that the first testimonies to the presence of the risen Christ encounter both faith and no faith. It is said that even some of those who are directly confronted with the appearance of the risen Christ doubt. For example, Matthew 28:17 reports that the disciples see the risen Christ and fall down before him. But then the text explicitly says: "But some doubted." Along the same lines, Luke 24:36-37 reports: "While they were talking about this, Jesus himself stood among them and said to them, 'Peace be with you.' They were startled and terrified, and thought that they were seeing a ghost." The Gospel of John also follows this "resurrection logic." John 20:19 and 20:26 emphasize that Jesus comes and joins the disciples "while the doors were shut."

This remarkable connection between presence to the senses and appearance is most strikingly presented in the Emmaus story. Luke 24:16 reports that at first when Jesus joins the disciples along the way, "their eyes were kept from recognizing him." Luke 24:31 then makes clear that which is characteristic of the recognition of the risen Christ: recognition of the risen Christ by means of the senses and the withdrawal of the risen Christ belong together. To be sure, after Jesus had broken the bread, "their eyes were opened." But in the very act of their thus recognizing him, "he vanished from their sight."

In manifold ways, the resurrection reports of personal encounters contradict the impression that the resurrection only restores the old pre-Easter vitality and corporeality of Jesus of Nazareth. "Resurrection" does not mean: The dead Jesus rises up again and leaves his grave as if nothing had happened. Jesus' resurrection does not simply lead to a continuation of a merely interrupted earthly life. It is not a mere reentry into the life lived prior to death. The risen Christ does not continue to live with his disciples and fellow humans in the way that they live and interact with each other. There is no place in the Bible where a person says: "How good that you're here again, Jesus!" Rather, coming into contact with the Risen One is experienced as a revelation of God, a theophany. The disciples and the women throw themselves to the ground. "Doubting Thomas" calls out: "My Lord and my God!" (Jn 20:28). And repeatedly the text says: "But some doubted." Yet what kind of reality is this new life and this new corporeality?

The biblical texts confront us with a tension with which modern common sense is not the first to have extreme difficulties. (More precisely, today's common sense has no trouble with this tension between presence to the senses and appearance when common sense meets it in the media. Who today would have difficulty letting a human being on the screen pass as a "real person"?) The biblical resurrection texts confront us with the complicated interconnection between the sensuous reality and the appearance of the risen Christ. How are we to understand this tension between presence to the senses and presence in the mode of appearance? How are we to grasp the new corporeality and vitality of the resurrection?

The testimonies to the resurrection make it necessary to call simplistic notions of "reality" into question. These testimonies very consciously provoke the question: Were the perceptions of the risen Christ nothing but offspring of the fantasy of individual human beings? At the same time, however, these testimonies work against the suspicion that these persons had succumbed to illusions in their encounter with the risen Christ. On the one hand, the texts give rise to the suspicion that Jesus' appearance was an illusion. On the other hand, they want to undermine this suspicion.

By insisting on the disconcerting interconnection between the sensuous character and the appearance of the risen Christ, the testimonies to the resurrection emphasize that the resurrection reality is more than a merely natural event. This reality touches us more deeply and is more powerful than merely natural events. Here we are dealing not merely with the earthly human being who could be crucified and killed. Here we meet the resurrected Christ, who has overcome death. Here we have before us not a merely earthly human being, who can be present only at one place in space and time. Here we meet the resurrected and exalted Christ, who can and does reveal himself in many locations at the same time, "in another form" and in surprising ways. But this resurrection reality is not a fleeting figure of fantasy or an illusion. It is attested by many witnesses, in many different experiential contexts. The biblical testimonies name this a presence "in the Spirit." However, "in the Spirit" does not mean: only in thoughts, or even only in illusions. "In the Spirit" means: in a fullness of recollections, expectations, and experiences.

The recognition of Jesus' resurrection is no more an illusion than is the discovery of justice or of mathematics. But this event is also not only the discovery of a new order and truth. Rather, here Jesus makes himself present and active in a new way. In the resurrection, his pre-Easter person and his pre-Easter life continue in a new way: Looking from the outside, one could speak of a cultural-historical event. Not Jesus' biological body, but Jesus' person and life, which this body carried, seek and find in the witnesses of the resurrection a new body as carrier of the earthly-historical existence of Jesus Christ. Yet how can we make clear that this is not merely the result of a sudden change of mind induced by psychosis or trickery, or of a contagious fantasy?

What grows out of the multiplicity of testimonies to the presence of the risen Jesus is not simply the reconstruction of the "that" of his having come (Bultmann), or only the reconstruction of a "life of Jesus." There occurs an unfolding of the fullness of life of the pre-Easter Jesus, with his utterances and his intentions and, in all this, a rich and lively knowledge and glorification of his person in its continued effectiveness. The accounts that use encounters with the appearing Christ to testify to the resurrection speak of a "living memory" or "living remembrance" being kindled by the presence of Jesus. This living memory occurs not merely as the act of recollecting, but also as the acts of experiencing, testifying, and expecting. (In what follows I deliberately speak of "living memory" or "living remembrance," although I could also say "faith." Cf. chapter 8.)[14]

The breaking of bread, the wounds, the forms of address, and the opening of the "scriptures" kindle the recognition of the presence of the Risen One and a living memory. One can imagine a multiplicity of further events that can set in motion the living memory of Jesus Christ. One

14. There are two reasons for highlighting this aspect of faith so strongly. First, I want to supply a christological corrective to the fuzzy and vacuous modern understanding of "faith." Second, I want to draw attention from the perspective of cross and resurrection to the depths of Jesus' charge: "Do this in remembrance of me."

example would be devoting attention to children or to people who are sick, suffering, or possessed. Another would be table fellowship that accepts persons who are excluded, who break taboos, or who are subjected to the strictures of taboo. Again, "Jesus' politico-symbolic conflicts"[15] with the temple cult and with the Roman Empire, and similar conflicts in historically analogous constellations, can also kindle the living memory of the risen Christ. With Jesus' new interpretation of *torah* and his proclamation of the coming reign of God, complex normative fields accrue to this living memory. Jesus' act of laying claim to intimate communion with God the creator and to the power to forgive sins brings further religious dimensions into this living memory. This living memory can go forth from such features of the historical Jesus, and in the interplay of various forms and contents, this living memory can give expression to the vitality and presence of the risen Christ. In the risen Christ, the whole fullness of Jesus' life is present with its creative power. *The divine miracle is not the revivification of an earthly life, but the presence of the fullness of the life of Jesus Christ in the resurrection.*

What for the outsider may be only an interesting cultural development, or perhaps a dismaying one, is anything but a luxury item for those who believe. They see growing out of *this* presence and out of *this* living memory those powers which actualize the reality intended by God. In the presence of the risen Christ, God's powers of creation and new creation are actualized in the midst of realities of social, cultural, and historical life that are jeopardized and self-jeopardizing. The great expectations of faith become clear and compelling when we put ourselves back into the many situations of conflict and distress into which and against which Jesus directed his message of the coming reign of God. They become clear and compelling when we call to mind the tensions between the Roman empire and those cultural and religious traditions of Israel that apparently were not up to the challenge of encountering the global power of Rome. It is above all the crucifixion that provides the context for answering the question of why such great expectations have over and over been placed in the renewing power of the presence of the risen Christ and in his living memory (see esp. chapters 2 and 6).

The remarkable and tension-ridden reality of the risen Christ compels

15. See the excellent article by Gerd Theipen, "Jesus und die symbolpolitischen Konflikte seiner Zeit: Sozialgeschichtliche Aspekte der Jesusforschung," *Evangelische Theologie* 57 (1997): 378-400.

us to ask: How can we relate appropriately to this complicated and offensive reality of the resurrection? The answer is: in the celebration of the Supper!

The Supper centers on a complex, sensuous process in which the risen and exalted Christ becomes present. The Supper gives Christians a form in which they can perceive the risen and exalted Christ with all their senses. The compact, sensuous perception (mediated by the giving and taking, the eating and drinking of bread and wine) bears the experience of the reality of the exalted Christ. At the same time the limits of merely sensuous experience are consciously noted.

For me, these insights indicated a way to answer the question "What happens in holy communion?"

- In doing so, it makes sense to begin by examining those aspects of the Supper which are accessible to general experience. This occurs in the first part of this book: *Holy Communion: Human Beings Thank God and Symbolically Celebrate a Community Meal in a Jeopardized World.* We will see that the Supper is a symbolic meal in a jeopardized and self-jeopardizing world, but a meal in which the reconciliation of human beings with God and the reconciliation of human beings with each other are celebrated.
- We must then seek to understand the way in which the risen and exalted Christ is "present" in this celebration. This is the task of the second part of the book: *Holy Communion — Celebration of the Presence of Jesus Christ.* There we will be concerned not only with the fullness of the presence of the resurrected Jesus Christ — a fullness which is hard to understand — but also a whole series of matters that are causes of offense today (self-giving, sacrifice, forgiveness of sins, the "return" of Christ, etc.).
- On these foundations, finally, we can in the third part clarify why the Supper has such great significance in Christian churches: *Holy Communion — Feast of the Church of All Times and Regions of the World, Celebration of Peace and of the New Creation, and Joyful Glorification of the Triune God.*

In the course of this investigation it will become evident why certain ways and forms of celebrating holy communion have an edifying, empowering, festive, and creative effect, while others leave the impression of a "sad colloquy." Clear answers will appear not only to the so-called "big theological questions," but also to very concrete, practical questions about the actual celebration of the Supper. On what basis, however, can we carry out this investigation?

The Power of the Biblical Texts

When we seek orientation in answering the question "What happens in holy communion?" three foundations stand out.

- The often discussed contributions of the Reformers and of the Counter Reformation to the theology of the Supper. Their advantage is that they are interested in clearly delineating the positions of the churches and confessions over against one another.
- The documents and results of the ecumenical discussions of recent decades. Their advantage is that, in the effort to understand the significance of the Supper, these discussions have engaged in an intensive search for commonalities in the midst of diverse church traditions and theologies. In the process they have developed a new style of coming to an understanding and new strategies for engaging in conversation. As a result we can even speak of exemplary contributions to ecumenical peace.
- The most important and ultimately normative foundation is provided by the biblical traditions. Both the Reformation and Counter Reformation as well as the ecumenical discussion of the last third of the twentieth century, which is particularly important to this book, appeal not only to the various traditions of ecclesial doctrinal formation and of liturgical practice, but also and especially to the biblical traditions, which are common to all of them. Again and again it is emphasized that the "biblical origins," and the celebrations of the Supper as they are attested there, must be normative for any understanding reached between churches, for church doctrine, and for ecclesial practice.[16] This state of affairs in itself makes it well-advised to choose in the first instance for this book, too, a basic orientation that is biblical.

16. See, e.g., "Windsor Statement" 1971 [A-RC], p. 69; "The Presence of Christ" 1977 [R-RC], pp. 449ff.; "The Eucharist" 1978 [L-RC], pp. 192ff.; "Baptism, Eucharist and Ministry" 1982 [WCC], pp. 466ff.

In addition, as we shall see, the biblical perspectives are richer and more differentiated than the other basic orientations.

- They introduce important viewpoints that even the encompassing ecumenical discussions on the global level have not taken into account, or at least have not done so sufficiently (see esp. chapters 2, 6, and 10).
- They do not fall victim to the mistake of theorizing about aspects of the Supper in abstraction from the actual celebration of the Supper, in abstraction from the community celebrating the Supper, or in abstraction from the Supper's "place in church life" (cf. esp. chapters 3, 4, 8, and 9).
- They stay with fruitful, creative tensions and differences, where ecclesial and theological debates have insisted on an "either-or" (see esp. chapters 5, 7, and 10).

For those reasons, almost all the chapters of this book explicitly take up perspectives of the biblical traditions and place them center stage. Most of these biblical perspectives are also found in the holy communion liturgies of the various churches. It is in the light of these biblical perspectives that Reformation, pre-Reformation, Counter Reformation, and recent ecumenical questions and insights, differences and commonalities come to expression.

This book will attempt not to give in to what continues to be a widespread tendency of both systematic and practical theologians: the tendency to move as quickly as possible to homogenize the biblical perspectives, to trace them back — or more precisely, to trim them back — to a single principle, one rule, one insight that is as short and as plausible as possible. Instead this book aims to show over against this reductionism that it is precisely together that the diverse biblical perspectives generate a clear and dramatically textured picture! Precisely in their reciprocal supplementation, their overlaps, and even their differences, the biblical perspectives offer, as we shall see, a rich, complex, and coherent picture of what happens in the Supper. This biblical-theological procedure, which cautiously develops a mosaic or a network of insights, has proved itself in the investigation of various themes of the Christian faith.[17] This book

17. See, e.g. — along with the article on resurrection mentioned in note 13 — M. Welker, *God the Spirit,* trans. John F. Hoffmeyer (Minneapolis: Fortress, 1994);

will also follow this procedure in order to answer the question "What happens in holy communion?"

Accordingly, the various "lights" of the biblical traditions concerning the Supper are to complement one another. Whoever blocks out some or many of these lights — perhaps because too much light seems to disturb the search for a simple principle or a simple, catchy answer — must be content with illusions of clarity, and is in fact casting about in murky waters indeed. Moreover, the diverse lights of the biblical traditions and their collaboration also make it possible to recognize the great steps forward in recent decades in ecumenical agreement concerning the Supper. In light of the biblical texts, insights of the churches which in times past were presented as standing in opposition to one another can be recognized as diverse perspectives on a rich content of faith. This content of faith is simultaneously complex and clear. In all its clarity it is so rich and fruitful that it cannot be grasped in one simple, short formula.

Along the way on which this book embarks, many, indeed most of the positions of the various churches which in times past were set up as rigid differences against each other, and which led to mutual condemnations, will be placed in overarching perspectives. It will become possible to recognize them as mutual enrichments in the shared search for the truth. It will become clear that differences are not simply something bad, but rather that differences can be fruitful; that they need not lead to conflicts, but rather that under certain presuppositions they can form creative contrasts.[18] In making the effort to uncover these creative contrasts in differences, this book continues the path embarked upon by the global ecu-

---

M. Welker, *Creation and Reality,* trans. John F. Hoffmeyer (Minneapolis: Fortress, 1999); M. Welker, "The Reign of God," *Theology Today* 49 (1992): 500-515. Regarding the method employed, cf. M. Welker, "Biblische Theologie. Fundamentaltheologisch," *Die Religion in Geschichte und Gegenwart,* vol. 1, 4th ed. (Tübingen, 1998), pp. 1549-53; Bernd Oberdorfer, "Biblisch-realistische Theologie," in Sigrid Brandt and Bernd Oberdorfer, eds., *Resonanzen: Theologisch Beiträge* (Michael Welker zum 50. Geburtstag) (Wuppertal: Foedus, 1997), pp. 63-83.

18. The great mathematician, natural scientist, and philosopher Alfred North Whitehead repeatedly called attention to the task of philosophy, art, and the sciences to transform differences and conflicts into creative contrasts. Cf. M. Welker, *Universalität Gottes und Relativität der Welt: Theologische Kosmologie im Dialog mit dem amerikanschen Prozepdenken nach Whitehead,* 2nd ed. (Neukirchen: Neukirchener, 1988); Michael Hampe, *Alfred North Whitehead* (Munich: Beck, 1998).

menical dialogues of recent decades — including those on the theme of eucharist and Supper.

From Conflicts Between Churches to Ecumenical Understanding Concerning the Supper

Seen from the outside, the sequence of events in holy communion seems simple, but what is happening in the process is complex and rich. Many of the past controversies between the larger churches can be traced back to the richness of this process. Again and again, individual aspects and moments of the complex process were emphasized at the expense of other aspects and moments. In this way, distorted images arose — distorted images of the Supper and distorted images of the positions of the other churches.

In the last decades of the twentieth century, the ecumenical conversations of the larger churches concerning the Supper have in part disentangled this jumble of conflictual relations, and in part left it behind. A new climate has arisen, in which the churches' various understandings of the Supper, in relations of mutual complementarity, have grown together into a differentiated perception of rich and lively contents of faith. As a rule, the truths recognized by the individual churches were not abandoned and betrayed, but often more clearly propounded. A new style of conversation was normative for this new climate. This style of conversation can be characterized as follows:

1. All ecumenical conversations in recent decades concerning holy communion begin by asking: What are the relative commonalities in theological knowledge and ecclesial practice? Once commonalities in theology and practice have been sought and found, the remaining differences are treated in light of these commonalities.[19]

19. Among Protestant and German-speaking churches, the Lutheran-Reformed dialogue concerning the Supper certainly provided the primary model in this regard. This dialogue was initially sought in the shared straits of the Confessing Church. After the Second World War it was continued and extended to other European countries. The following were milestones along the way: the "Declaration of the Second Session of the Fourth Confessing Synod of the Evangelical Church of the Old Prussian Union" in Halle in 1937; the "Arnoldshain Theses on the Supper" (1957) and the "Clarifications" of these theses (1962); and the "Leuenberg Agreement" of 1973. See the excellent introductory presentation by Lessing, *Abendmahl*, pp. 19-41.

2. If the previous conflicts and mutual condemnations are treated in light of relative commonalities, it becomes possible to deal with historical differences in a subtle and multilayered way. Some differences can be completely abandoned because they prove to be erroneous or outdated. Other differences are perceived as fruitful, differing perspectives or as helpful contrasts that make possible a better grasp of the complexity and vitality of the shared content of faith.[20] Finally, in light of the commonalities and fruitful contrasts, the remaining differences can appear as particularly precarious and burdensome. Yet in this light these differences can be regarded as challenges to continue with persistence the search for further and deeper commonalities.[21]
3. In order to do what is possible to exclude one-sided perspectives and overly rapid harmonizations from the process of ascertaining commonalities and differences, the churches normally take care to insure that conversation partners and commission members come "from many countries" and represent "a wide variety of theological backgrounds."[22]

In this differentiated commonality, the ecumenical conversations of recent decades have been able to elucidate the rich and complex process of holy communion better than was possible in times of emphatic confessional controversies. In this way these ecumenical conversations represent contributions to ecumenical peace and are a particular blessing of the twentieth century. In what follows we shall take up these "contributions to ecumenical peace." We shall try to clarify and supplement them. In the process it should become clear that holy communion is a driving force for ecumenical peace not only in the Supper's liturgical practice, as it is celebrated day after day, week after week, month after month, year after year in countless places all over the world. Also in the theological recognition of what happens in holy communion, the Supper can prove to be a source of "contributions to ecumenical peace."

20. In this regard a new biblical-theological orientation has frequently been normative in recent years: "A clearer understanding of the pluralist nature of New Testament Christianity . . . makes all claims to exclusiveness embarrassing to maintain" ("Pullach Report" 1972 [A-L], p. 31. Of course, such a position requires a clear differentiation between pluralism, diffuse "plurality," individualism, and relativism: cf. M. Welker, *Kirche im Pluralismus* (Gütersloh: Kaiser, 1995).

21. See "Facing Unity" 1984 [L-RC], pp. 20-24, for "models of comprehensive union" that all include a culture of fruitful differences.

22. "Windsor Statement" 1971 [A-RC], p. 68.

Despite — no, precisely because of — its ecumenical engagement, this book does not deny its evangelical profile, shaped by the theological tradition of the Reformation. Especially in chapters 1, 9, and 10, it will formulate genuinely Reformation insights on a biblical basis, and will commend these insights to ecumenical conversation partners. These insights concern in particular the character of the Supper as a meal, the carrying out of pastoral responsibility in the celebration of the Supper, the significance of the forgiveness of sins, and the problems surrounding the issue of mutual invitation or admission to table fellowship. Presumably at least the pre-Reformation churches will not accept these insights without hesitation and doubts. However, this book also attempts to give central concerns of these churches in the theology of the Supper a more just treatment than has been the case in some "typically Protestant" positions and pronouncements. Examples of such critical themes are: the perception of the breadth of the ecumenical church over against the mere concentration on the "gathered community"; the respect for the concern for the responsible celebration of the sacrament, as that concern arises in the theology of the office of ministry; and the correction of an overly narrow understanding of the "memory of Christ."

This book will engage the richness and the manifold influence of holy communion from twelve perspectives. Yet despite singing the praises of holy communion, we must also ultimately recognize its modest place in the upbuilding of the church through God's word and God's Spirit. The Supper is an important point of concentration and a foundational source in the life of the church. But its celebration far from exhausts the church's mission and commission. Precisely when we learn with good reason to attach great value to the Supper, we will learn to guard against overvaluing it. We will expect a lot of it. But we will not overburden it with claims and expectations. In attempting to elucidate the richness of what happens in holy communion, this book also aims at a sober perception of the Supper: it is not the sole source and not the sole high point of ecclesial life; it is not the sole basis and the sole criterion for the renewal of the church!

Since this book is directed not only at theologians, but intends to be generally accessible, reference to literature belonging to the theological discipline is minimal, and occurs almost exclusively in the notes. An appendix — "Documents of the 'Growth in Agreement' of Churches on the Global Level in Questions of Holy Communion, in Chronological Order, 1931-1990" — is intended to enable and ease the process of becoming oriented in the more comprehensive ecumenical conversation. The individual chapters are written in such a way that it is possible to plunge directly into various themes, problems, and points of view, without having read all that precedes in a linear fashion. Summaries at the end of the individual chapters are also intended to enable a selective reading that is looking for information and counsel only concerning specific questions regarding the theme of holy communion.

PART 1

Holy Communion: Human Beings Thank God and Symbolically Celebrate a Community Meal in a Jeopardized World

CHAPTER 1

"Do This . . ." Who Is Supposed to Do What?

Symbolic Community Meal — or Merely a Preparation for That Meal?

What happens in holy communion? The first of the answers to this question is: *A symbolic community meal is celebrated by a meal community, a table fellowship.*[1] This answer sounds cumbersome. But it ought to make clear that holy communion:

- is not only and not essentially the mere preparation for or the mere offer of a community meal;
- is also not only the gathering of a community that is ready for the meal.

The recognition that in holy communion a gathered community celebrates a symbolic community meal is indispensable — and, as we will see, has major consequences!

To be sure, the Supper is not simply a meal to sate hunger. For good reasons, what is celebrated is a "liturgical meal employing symbolic words and actions."[2] Yet this recognition, for which more precise arguments must be given, must not lead to separating the preparation for the celebration of the meal from the actual event of the community meal. It must not mislead us

1. I have taken the phrase from the title of Matthias Klinghardt's book *Gemeinschaftsmahl und Mahlgemeinschaft: Soziologie und Liturgie frühchristlicher Mahlfeiern,* TANZ 13 (Tübingen: Francke, 1996), cited as Klinghardt, *Gemeinschaftsmahl.*

2. "Baptism, Eucharist and Ministry" 1982 [WCC], p. 475.

into assuming that in principle we have satisfactorily celebrated the Supper by concentrating on the mere preparation for the celebration of a meal.

The Sacrifice of the Mass and Communion — the Sacrifice of the Mass Also Without Communion? The Traditional Roman Catholic Position

Roman Catholicism played the primary role in dividing holy communion into two parts: the *sacrifice of the mass* and the *communion.* The upshot was the division and then the separation of:

1. the so-called sacrifice of the mass, in which the meal is prepared for by the consecration of bread and wine, in which the bread and wine are changed *(transubstantiation)* into Christ's body and blood;
2. the communion, in which the meal (i.e., as a rule only the "consecrated bread") is distributed to the congregation and eaten.

This separation in the process of holy communion may at first seem insignificant. But it has major consequences for the understanding and the practice of the Supper. In order to know whether the differentiation or even separation between the sacrifice of the mass and the communion is helpful and permissible, or problematic, we ask: With the words "Do this in remembrance of me," what is Jesus Christ actually charging the disciples to do?

- Is he charging the disciples to carry out the shared celebration of the meal, as he carries it out with them? If so, then in no way may "sacrifice of the mass" and "communion" be separated from one another!
- Or is he charging them to consecrate bread and wine, so that bread and wine are transformed into Christ's body and blood? Is he charging them, therefore, to prepare a special meal by the consecration and transformation of bread and wine, in order to make possible in this way a shared meal celebration? Taken for itself and independently of the communion, does that which is called the "consecration" correspond to Christ's commission?

If the latter is true, then the sacrifice of the mass can also be carried out without the communion. The sacrifice of the mass (in which the consecration and transubstantiation take place) would be the basic event, the decisive process in the Supper. It would stand on its own. Of course, one could still admit that the Supper certainly aims toward the communion. But the basis of the celebration of the meal, and thus the decisive event of the Supper, would lie in the "sacrifice of the mass." In principle, the sacrifice of the mass would be self-sufficient. The communion could not be carried out without the sacrifice of the mass, but the sacrifice of the mass could indeed be carried out without the communion.

If this were correct and materially fitting, one could also understand why in Roman Catholicism so-called private and solitary masses (*missa privata* = a mass requested by private persons or held for their own devotion; *missa solitaria* = a mass held by the priest alone) are considered valid. It would also be simple enough to make sense of the veneration of the consecrated and transformed "elements" of bread and wine outside of the celebration of the Supper, which is still customary today in parts of Catholicism (so-called "tabernacle piety"). What basically happens in holy communion would be the transformation of the "elements" of bread and wine in the process of the consecration. Within the framework of the sacrifice of the mass, the so-called transubstantiation would be central and normative.

Important consequences of this view are:

- The celebration of the Supper is not necessarily dependent on the presence of the community!
- The eating of a shared, symbolic meal is not an essential component of holy communion. For this reason the expression "eucharist" (thanksgiving) is readily employed for holy communion.
- Giving and taking, the charge to eat and drink, the eating and drinking themselves, and in general the meal community and the symbolic community meal are in principle dispensable according to this view, since the decisive event is "the consecration" or "the transubstantiation."

In the normative doctrinal documents of the Roman Catholic Church,[3] one repeatedly finds in the sections dealing with holy commu-

3. Here they will be cited according to John F. Clarkson et al., eds. and trans., *The Church Teaches: Documents of the Church in English Translation* (St. Louis: B. Herder, 1955). Numbers refer not to pages, but to marginal numbers assigned to sections by the editors.

nion or the eucharist formulations such as: "The bread and the wine . . . are the true body and the true blood of our Lord Jesus Christ after the consecration."[4] The formulation of the 13th session (1551) of the great council of the Counter Reformation, the Council of Trent, is very clear and very illuminating for the traditional Roman Catholic position: "For before the apostles received the Eucharist from the hands of our Lord [see Mt 26:26; Mk 14:22], he told them that it was his body that he was giving them."[5] Evidently this means that according to biblical tradition the "transubstantiation" of bread and wine occurred before the reception of the elements, and independently of that reception.

Eleven years later, in the 22d session (1562), in the "Canons on the Most Holy Sacrifice of the Mass," the council is logical and concise in formulating this statement of condemnation: "8. If anyone says that the Masses in which the priest alone communicates sacramentally, are illicit and should be done away with: let him be anathema."[6]

More than four hundred years later, on September 3, 1965, in the encyclical *Mysterium fidei,* Pope Paul VI reacts to visible difficulties with the theology and practice of the sacrifice of the mass — even among the Roman Catholic clergy. Paul VI tells the "Venerable Brothers" that "some of those who are dealing with this Most Holy Mystery in speech and writing are disseminating opinions on Masses celebrated in private or on the dogma of transubstantiation that are disturbing the minds of the faithful. . . ." Then the pope calls the problems by name:

> To give an example of what We are talking about, it is not permissible to extol the so-called "community" Mass in such a way as to detract from Masses that are celebrated privately . . . or, finally, to propose and act upon the opinion that Christ Our Lord is no longer present

4. Clarkson et al., *The Church Teaches,* p. 713; cf. pp. 712, 715, 719 and *passim.*

5. Clarkson et al., *The Church Teaches,* p. 721. As the text proceeds, Trent insists: "There can be no doubt, then, that the faithful of Christ, in accordance with the perpetual custom of the Catholic Church, venerate this most holy Sacrament with the worship of latria which is due to the true God. . . . Nor is this Sacrament to be the less adored because it was instituted by Christ to be received (see Matt. 26:26ff.). For in this Sacrament we believe that the same God is present whom the eternal Father brought into the world, saying of him: 'And let all the angels of God adore him' (Heb. 1:6; see Ps. 96:7)" (Clarkson et al., *The Church Teaches,* p. 723.

6. Clarkson et al., *The Church Teaches,* p. 763.

in the consecrated Hosts that remain after the celebration of the sacrifice of the Mass has been completed.[7]

In making his case, Paul VI essentially appeals to "the tradition" and to the fact that the "formulas . . . that the Church used to propose the dogmas of faith" are not timebound, "but are adapted to all men of all times and all places." For this reason, the pope holds, they must not be relativized by a particular culture, a particular instance of scientific progress, or particular theological innovations.[8] He does not address the conflicts with the biblical material.

However, the positions criticized by the pope do not owe their existence to a way of thinking that attempts to line up with a mere spirit of the age. They do not owe their existence to an effort to swim with the currents of twentieth-century fashion. Instead, as we shall see, the position of the Council of Trent, which Paul VI is trying to maintain and defend, stands in hopeless conflict with the biblical texts. It thereby also stands in conflict with the very fruitful and exemplary biblical-exegetical orientation of Catholic theology after the Second Vatican Council (1962-65). The positions criticized by the pope have therefore gained increasingly clear acceptance in the ecumenical discussions of the twentieth century, *including on the side of the Catholic church.* Only by ignoring the biblical texts can one hold the view of the council of the Counter Reformation: "For before the apostles received the Eucharist from the hands of our Lord, he told them that it was his body that he was giving them." One cannot hold that view if one takes the biblical texts seriously.[9]

7. "Mysterium fidei," in Claudia Carlen, ed., *The Papal Encyclicals: 1958-1981* (Wilmington, N.C.: McGrath, 1981), p. 166.

8. "Mysterium fidei," p. 168.

9. Cf. the very cautious critique by Herbert Vorgrimler, *Sakramententheologie,* Leitfaden Theologie 17 (Düsseldorf: Patmos, 1987), pp. 191-92 and 215ff. Helmut Feld, *Das Verständnis des Abendmahls,* Erträge der Forschung 50 (Darmstadt: Wissenschaftliche Buchgesellschaft, 1976), pp. 123ff., also emphasizes that, for the discussion of the Supper and for the enlivening of ecumenical conversation, looking to the biblical texts for orientation has become the normative practice.

What Do the Biblical Texts Support?

Mark 14 explicitly places the statement that is decisive for this question — "This is my body" — after the distribution of the bread and the invitation: "Take the bread" (14:22). And in Mark 14:24, the declaration "This is my blood" follows only "after" the drinking from the cup — indeed, after "all of them drank from it," as the text explicitly says.

> **Mark 14:22-24:**
>
> While they were eating, he took a loaf of bread, and after blessing it he broke it, gave it to them, and said, "Take; this is my body." Then he took a cup, and after giving thanks he gave it to them, and all of them drank from it. He said to them, "This is my blood of the covenant, which is poured out for many."

In Matthew 26, too, the breaking and distribution of the bread, as well as the invitation "Take and eat," precede the identification of the bread with the body of Christ (Mt 26:26). The parallel is true for the gift of the cup.

> **Matthew 26:26-28:**
>
> While they were eating, Jesus took a loaf of bread, and after blessing it he broke it, gave it to the disciples, and said, "Take, eat; this is my body." Then he took a cup, and after giving thanks he gave it to them, saying, "Drink from it, all of you; for this is my blood of the covenant, which is poured out for many for the forgiveness of sins."

Luke 22:19 also explicitly connects the distribution of the broken bread with the identification: "This is my body, which is given for you."

> **Luke 22:19-20:**
>
> Then he took a loaf of bread, and when he had given thanks, he broke it and gave it to them, saying, "This is my body, which is given for you. Do this in remembrance of me." And he did the same with the cup after supper, saying, "This cup that is poured out for you is the new covenant in my blood."

Finally, Paul also does not support the separation of a preceding act of so-called consecration from a succeeding act — possibly to be omitted — of breaking and distributing, taking and eating the bread.

It is revealing that 1 Corinthians 10:16b reads: "The bread that we break, is it not a sharing in the body of Christ?" One could object: The breaking of the bread is not its distribution! And since 1 Corinthians 11:24 also emphasizes only the breaking of the bread before the identification: "This is my body that is for you," one could suspect here the basis for a possible cleft between the preparation for the meal and the actual event of the meal. But arguing against this suspicion is 1 Corinthians 11:25, where what would be the so-called consecration of the cup is interlaced with the eating of the meal as an already done deed.

> **1 Corinthians 11:23-26:**
>
> For I received from the Lord what I also handed on to you, that the Lord Jesus on the night when he was betrayed took a loaf of bread, and when he had given thanks, he broke it and said, "This is my body that is for you. Do this in remembrance of me." In the same way he took the cup also, after supper [literally: after they had eaten], saying, "This cup is the new covenant in my blood. Do this, as often as you drink it, in remembrance of me." For as often as you eat this bread and drink the cup, you proclaim the Lord's death until he comes.

Only "after they had eaten" is the cup explicitly characterized as "the new covenant in my blood." Thus the tradition that Paul claims to have "received from the Lord" also makes it impossible to separate a consecration of bread and wine from the act of communal eating and drinking.

Finally, 1 Corinthians 11:26 also makes clear that it is an erroneous departure from the biblical traditions to separate one part of the event of the Supper from the communal eating and drinking, and to treat that one separated part as central and decisive. In verse 26 we read: "For as often as you eat this bread and drink the cup, you proclaim the Lord's death until he comes."[10] This means, however, that there is no biblical basis for disengaging the identification of body and bread, wine and blood from the breaking of the bread, the distribution, and the communal eating and drinking.

This has been emphasized not only by the concluding reports of the intra-Protestant conversations on the Supper, initially concentrated in Germany and other parts of Europe: for example, the 1957 "Arnoldshain

10. See in detail chapter 6. Cf. Miguel Garijo-Guembe, "Die Eucharistie nach römisch-katholischem Verständnis," in M. Garijo-Guembe, J. Rohls, and G. Wenz, *Mahl des Herrn: Ökumenische Studien* (Frankfurt: Lembeck, 1988), pp. 9ff., 65.

Theses on the Supper," the subsequent clarifications published in 1962, and the "Leuenberg Agreement" of 1973.

The global ecumenical conversations, in which Protestant, Orthodox, and Roman Catholic (authorized by Rome!) theologians and church leaders collaborated, have also in recent decades emphasized with increasing clarity that the Supper is essentially a community meal.

Unanimity among the Reformation, Post-Reformation, and Orthodox Churches: "The Supper Is an Act of Worship of the Community Gathered in Jesus' Name"

The Arnoldshain Theses on the Supper (1957) have been very important for the subsequent course of ecumenical conversations. The third thesis clearly states: "The Supper is an act of worship of the community gathered in Jesus' name." Thesis 3.3 then gives a succinct description of the external process of the Supper: "With prayer, praise, and thanksgiving, bread and wine are taken, the Lord's words of institution are spoken, and bread and wine are given to the congregation to eat and to drink."[11]

Various Protestant churches were invited to take a position on these theses. The churches reacted not only with agreement, but also with critical questions. These questions concerned, among other things, the consecration of the elements of bread and wine. Had the Arnoldshain theses not given sufficient attention and attached sufficient value to this process, which is so important for Roman Catholicism?

In order to respond to the positions taken by the churches, a "Concluding Report" with clarifications of the Arnoldshain theses was published in 1962, after renewed and intensive consultations. The clarification to thesis 3 says that "through the actual celebration of holy communion, as described in thesis 3.3, bread and wine are set apart and placed in the service of this meal. On the basis of exegesis of New Testament texts, the signatories of this report do not feel that they are able to require in addition a particular act of consecration. Nor do they find themselves able to reckon a particular doctrine of consecration among those things which are 'essential to the understanding of the essence, gift, and reception of the Supper.'"[12]

11. *Arnoldshain,* p. 65.

12. *Arnoldshain,* pp. 72-73. Cf. Lessing, *Abendmahl,* esp. pp. 32ff.

The Leuenberg Agreement, the 1973 joint declaration of the Reformation churches in Europe, emphasizes the communal character of the celebration of the Supper. This comes through with particular clarity in thesis 19: "We cannot separate communion with Jesus Christ in his body and blood from the act of eating and drinking. To be concerned about the manner of Christ's presence in the Lord's Supper in abstraction from this act is to run the risk of obscuring the meaning of the Lord's Supper."[13]

The Reformation churches agree not only among themselves, but also with the Anglicans and with the Orthodox in the view that the Supper is essentially a communal meal, and that it is impossible to separate an act of consecration from the celebration of the meal. The "Pullach Report," which issued from dialogues between Anglicans and Lutherans, places the "real presence" of Christ in the unitary context of "eucharistic action (including consecrations) *and* reception."[14] The Anglican–Orthodox "Moscow Statement" of 1976 needs only a few words to emphasize that "the consecration of the bread and wine results from the whole sacramental liturgy."[15] This means, though, that it is inadmissible to separate sacrifice of the mass, consecration, and transubstantiation of the elements, on the one hand, from communion, celebration of the meal, and participation of the gathered community, on the other hand.

The Cautious Change in the Roman Catholic Position in the Last Third of the Twentieth Century

The interconfessional conversations on the global level in which the Roman Catholic Church has participated have for years now been moving toward statements of similar clarity. This belongs to the great, indeed quietly revolutionary events of ecumenical understanding in the twentieth century.

We find the following formulation already in the Methodist–Roman Catholic "Denver Report" of 1971: "Bread and wine do not mean the same outside the context of the Eucharistic celebration as they do within that context. Within the Eucharistic celebration they become the sign par excellence of Christ's redeeming presence to His people. . . . The perfect

13. *Leuenberg,* p. 149.
14. "Pullach Report" 1972 [A-L]; p. 23; emphasis added.
15. "Moscow Statement" 1976 [A-O], p. 46.

participation in the celebration of the Eucharist is the communion of the faithful."[16]

The Anglican–Roman Catholic "Windsor Statement" of 1971 is still clearer: "The Lord's words at the last supper, 'Take and eat; this is my body,' do not allow us to dissociate the gift of the presence and the act of sacramental eating."[17]

New ground is broken by the 1978 report "The Eucharist" from the Joint Roman Catholic–Lutheran Commission established by the Secretariat for Promoting Christian Unity in Rome and by the Lutheran World Federation. The same is true of the Anglican–Roman Catholic "Elucidation" issued in Salisbury in 1979 concerning eucharistic doctrine.

The document "The Eucharist" notes "the shared conviction that the Eucharist has the character of a meal,"[18] and explicitly emphasizes that "Lutherans and Catholics confess together the conviction that by its very essence the Eucharist is a communal meal."[19] The conclusions of the Salisbury text, written as an elucidation of the "Windsor Statement," read like a meaningful supplement to the position just quoted from "The Eucharist." The Salisbury "Elucidation" states: "If veneration [of the reserved elements] is wholly dissociated from the eucharistic celebration of the community it contradicts the true doctrine of the eucharist." The

16. "Denver Report" 1971 [M-RC], pp. 326-27.

17. "Windsor Statement" 1971 [A-RC], p. 71.

18. "Das Herrenmahl" 1978 [L-RC], Harding Meyer et al., eds., *Dokumente wachsender Übereinstimmung: Sämtliche Berichte und Konsenstexte interkonfessioneller Gespräche auf Weltebene,* vol. 1, rev. ed. (Paderborn: Bonifatius, 1991), p. 287. The citation is taken from the original German edition, since this particular line was inadvertently omitted in the process of printing the English version in the collection *Growth in Agreement* (see appendix).

19. "The Eucharist" 1978 [L-RC], p. 208. See also: "Since the Second Vatican Council a significant change has taken place in the liturgical practice of the Roman Catholic Church which underlines the superiority of the 'communal celebration involving the presence and active participation of the faithful . . . even though every Mass has of itself a public and social nature.' This priority of communal celebration signifies an important *rapprochement* in our eucharistic practice" (ibid.). See further: "Catholics and Lutherans are at one in the conviction that bread and wine belong to the complete form of the Eucharist. . . . The possibilities of receiving the Eucharist in both kinds have been considerably extended by the Second Vatican Council in regard to both the occasions and the communicants" (ibid.). Cf. Garijo-Guembe, "Die Eucharistie nach römisch-katholischem Verständnis," pp. 65ff.; Franz-Josef Nocke, *Sakramententheologie: Ein Handbuch* (Düsseldorf: Patmos, 1997), pp. 171ff.

judgment on tabernacle piety is drastic: "Any dissociation of such devotion from this primary purpose, which is communion in Christ of all his members, is a distortion in eucharistic practice."[20]

The biblically oriented Roman Catholic–Reformed consensus text "The Presence of Christ in Church and World" (1977) is hardly less clear in repeatedly highlighting the communal character of the celebration of the Supper. In this celebration "the new life of fellowship of Christendom is represented to the world." Catholics and Reformed jointly emphasize that "as often as we come together in the Church to obey our Lord's command to 'do this in *anamnesis* of me,' he is in our midst." They emphasize the connection between the gathering of God's people and the "sanctification" of bread and wine, and they assert that "the institution of the Eucharist constitutes the Church" as a "community of love."[21]

These and other statements in documentations of ecumenical conversations on the global level show a readiness in Roman Catholicism to turn gradually away from the custom of private and solitary masses, and from the isolated or one-sidedly emphasized sacrifice of the mass.[22] This process of turning away is accompanied by a diminution of tabernacle piety, by a reduction in the veneration of the "consecrated elements" even after the celebration of the Supper. (Sometimes it is emphasized that the meaning of the reservation of the consecrated elements is their distribution to persons who are sick and who could not participate in the shared celebration of the Supper.) Finally, this development is accompanied by the increasing recognition that the Supper should be celebrated "in both kinds" *(sub utraque,* not only *sub una):* that is, with bread *and* with wine. Normatively, the biblical texts and the new exegetical-theological orientation of Catholicism after Vatican II support and compel this new development. At the same time, as far as we are in a position to know, this devel-

20. "Eucharistic Doctrine: Elucidation" 1979 [A-RC], p. 76.

21. "The Presence of Christ" 1977 [R-RC], pp. 451-54. Cf. also the comment on the celebration of the Supper in the early church: "When the Christian community assembled with glad and generous hearts . . ." (p. 450).

22. See, e.g., "Facing Unity" 1984 [L-RC], p. 31: "Moreover, in its forms of piety, its liturgical life (celebration of Mass, for example), and its government (for example, by the general development of synodal elements at all levels of church life), the Catholic Church is reflecting on its origins, thereby showing concretely that in each of these areas it understands itself as a church in need of 'continual reformation.'" Concerning reforms in the practice of the mass, cf. "Facing Unity," p. 39.

opment also matches the trajectories of early Christian practice of the Supper until the third or fourth century.

The Early Church's Practice of the Supper: Unity of a Full Community Meal and a Symbolically Celebrated Meal

In his book *Community Meal and Meal Community,* Matthias Klinghardt posed the question: "How was it that early Christian communities gathered for communal meals that in some way or another were specifically religious?" In view of the multiformity of piety and of communities in early Christianity, it was by no means a foregone conclusion that "all Christian communities — in the most diverse areas of mission, with the most diverse theological profiles, from the most diverse backgrounds and traditions, and with a broad spectrum of social backgrounds . . . would gather for a meal."[23] On the basis of the evidence, Klinghardt comes to the conclusion that this practice had a long history in early Christianity. Only beginning in the third or fourth century did the communion *(koinonia)* of the community no longer consist of the assembly for a full communal meal. The community is no longer constituted by the concretely experienced meal community in communal eating and drinking, but in what Klinghardt calls the "community of eucharistic communication."[24]

While meal communion and communal meals are constitutive for the early Christian communities, the "eucharistic communion . . . is no longer (recognizably) tied to a full meal. The worship service takes place in the morning . . . and is marked . . . by a sequence in which reading and instruction precede the celebration of the eucharist."[25] Klinghardt emphasizes that the history of this change — away from a community meal to a community of religious communication, cut loose from the celebration of a meal — is not simple. But he also notes that historical and theological research has not yet sufficiently illuminated this development.[26]

23. Klinghardt, *Gemeinschaftsmahl und Mahlgemeinschaft,* p. 1.

24. Klinghardt, *Gemeinschaftsmahl,* p. 534.

25. Klinghardt, *Gemeinschaftsmahl,* p. 495.

26. In the last part of his book, Klinghardt himself offers some indications: "Liturgie und Soziologie des Mahls, *20: Vom Gemeinschaftsmahl zur Messe: Die Entwicklung im 2. Jh.," *Gemeinschaftsmahl,* pp. 499ff. Cf. also Robert Cabié, *The Eucharist,* vol. 2 of A. G. Martimort, ed., *The Church at Prayer: An Introduction to the Liturgy* (Collegeville, Minn.: Liturgical Press, 1986), pp. 13ff.

As we shall see in following chapters (especially chapters 2 and 5ff.), there are good reasons why the celebration of the Supper goes beyond a mere meal to satiate hunger. It made good sense to move consciously from a communal meal to satiate hunger to a symbolically celebrated meal, since in the center of this meal stand the presence of Jesus Christ, the deliverance and preservation of human beings in a threatened world, the glorification of God, and the elevation of humans to the status of bearers of God's presence. Moreover, holy communion is not only a meal of the concretely gathered community (see especially chapters 3, 8, and 9). Instead it binds together the gathered communities of the ecumenical church of all times and regions of the world. Yet in the midst of all efforts to bring to expression the particular character of this meal celebration, by no means can we lose sight of the traits of the communal meal (cf. especially chapters 3 and 4)! We must not distort or obscure the fact that the Supper is "an act of worship of the community gathered in Jesus' name," and that the symbolic giving and taking, the symbolic eating and drinking are indispensable components of the Supper!

There are, of course, numerous valid theological and practical reasons for the development in which the Christian church surrendered the connection between holy communion and a full meal ("agape" meal), and thereby came to celebrate the Supper as a symbolic meal. Yet wherever in this development the character of the communal meal is lost, wherever the concentration on a sacrifice of the mass separated from the gathered community and on a separate consecration threatens to obscure the meal community and the communal meal, there it is better to return to the early Christian connection of holy communion with a full meal.

The Supper is more than a meal to satiate hunger. The Supper is more than a meal of the concretely gathered community. But the interest in this "more" must not lead to "less" in practice. Wherever in a congregation, a church, a culture it becomes unclear that the holy communion is a symbolic communal meal of a meal community, the celebration of the Supper should at least occasionally be tied to the eating of an actual meal (agape meal).

Results

The Supper must be understood and celebrated as a symbolic communal meal. The biblical texts and the early Christian practice of the Supper argue against a concentration on the mere preparation for a meal (sacrifice of the mass, consecration, transubstantiation).

Of course, the Supper is more than a meal to satiate hunger (see especially chapters 3 and 9). It is a "liturgical meal employing symbolic words and actions" ("Baptism, Eucharist and Ministry").

However, "we cannot separate communion with Jesus Christ in his body and blood from the act of eating and drinking. To be concerned about the manner of Christ's presence in the Lord's Supper in abstraction from this act is to run the risk of obscuring the meaning of the Lord's Supper" (Leuenberg Agreement).

"Holy communion is an act of worship of the community gathered in Jesus' name" (Arnoldshain Theses on the Supper).

At the start of the twenty-first century, these biblically grounded insights are predominant in many ecumenical pronouncements of the larger churches on the global level concerning holy communion. Since Vatican II, the Roman Catholic Church has also been increasingly making these insights its own.

Where these insights are still being blocked or are again fading away, the Supper should at least occasionally be celebrated in connection with a full communal meal (agape meal).

CHAPTER 2

"In the Night in Which He Was Betrayed . . ."

Threatened Not Only from Outside, but Also from Inside!

What happens in holy communion? The second answer is: *Holy communion is instituted in the night in which Jesus Christ is betrayed and handed over to the powers of the world. It continually bears the imprint of this background.*

Amazingly, the ecumenical conversations have given practically no attention to this aspect. Precisely because most of the pronouncements are very nuanced and differentiated, it is all the more astounding that the "night in which he was betrayed" is notoriously left out of the picture. This fact carries major consequences. It leads to a situation in which the relation between the Supper and Passover is defined in a very unclear way, if an attempt to define it is made at all.[1] The texts relate the Passover meal and the celebration of the meal "in the night of self-giving and betrayal" only in vague and uncertain ways.[2] How do the Christian holy commu-

1. "The Eucharist" 1978 [L-RC] speaks of a "new passover meal," without further explanation. "Baptism, Eucharist and Ministry" says that "Christians see the eucharist prefigured in the Passover memorial. . . . It is the new paschal meal of the Church" ("Baptism, Eucharist and Ministry" 1982 [WCC], p. 475). *God's Reign and Our Unity* 1984 [A-R], p. 40, is very vague: "Like the Passover, the Eucharist is to be received as provision for an urgent journey (Ex 12:11)." Cf. Raymond Moloney, *The Eucharist,* Problems in Theology (Collegeville, Minn.: Liturgical Press, 1995), pp. 46ff.; Philippe Larere, *The Lord's Supper: Toward an Ecumenical Understanding of the Eucharist* (Collegeville, Minn.: Liturgical Press, 1993); Willy Rordorf et al., *The Eucharist of the Early Christians* (New York: Pueblo, 1978).

2. In the words of "The Presence of Christ" 1977 [R-RC], p. 449, "reflection on the

nion and the Jewish Passover meal hang together? We begin by asking: How are they different from each other?

The Participants in the Passover Meal: Threatened from Outside, but Committed in Solidarity to the Cause — the Participants in the Supper: Threatened from Outside and Self-Jeopardizing

It is no secret that the Passover meal is a meal of setting forth on the way: more precisely, a memorial celebration of the act of setting forth on the way out of slavery in Egypt. What is remembered is external affliction, external danger, preservation in this situation of distress, and liberation from it.

The Old Testament repeatedly summons the people to celebrate the Passover meal yearly in lively and sensuous remembrance of this event.

Exodus 12:1-10:

The LORD said to Moses and Aaron in the land of Egypt:

This month shall mark for you the beginning of months; it shall be the first month of the year for you.

Tell the whole congregation of Israel that on the tenth of this month they are to take a lamb for each family, a lamb for each household.

If a household is too small for a whole lamb, it shall join its closest neighbor in obtaining one; the lamb shall be divided in proportion to the number of people who eat of it.

Your lamb shall be without blemish, a year-old male; you may take it from the sheep or from the goats.

You shall keep it until the fourteenth day of this month; then the whole assembled congregation of Israel shall slaughter it at twilight.

---

celebration of the Eucharist must start from the biblical sources," and that means, among other things, "from the Old Testament background, particularly the Jewish Passover." Admittedly, the document does not meet this requirement. However, it does emphasize the theme of the forgiveness of sins more clearly than most other consensus texts (cf. p. 454). Lothar Lies points out structural parallels between the "offering of the Passover" and the "offering of the Supper" (*Eucharistie in ökumenischer Verantwortung* [Graz: Styria, 1996], pp. 159ff.).

> They shall take some of the blood and put it on the two doorposts and the lintel of the houses in which they eat it.
>
> They shall eat the lamb that same night; they shall eat it roasted over the fire with unleavened bread and bitter herbs.
>
> Do not eat any of it raw or boiled in water, but roasted over the fire, with its head, legs, and inner organs.
>
> You shall let none of it remain until the morning; anything that remains until the morning you shall burn.

The Passover is celebrated as a festival of setting forth, of setting forth in haste in the midst of great external affliction and distress.

> **Exodus 12:11-14:**
>
> This is how you shall eat it: your loins girded, your sandals on your feet, and your staff in your hand; and you shall eat it hurriedly. It is the passover of the LORD. For I will pass through the land of Egypt that night, and I will strike down every firstborn in the land of Egypt, both human beings and animals; on all the gods of Egypt I will execute judgments: I am the LORD. The blood shall be a sign for you on the houses where you live: when I see the blood, I will pass over you, and no plague shall destroy you. . . . This day shall be a day of remembrance for you. You shall celebrate it as a festival to the LORD; throughout your generations you shall observe it as a perpetual ordinance.

Several biblical texts pick up and shape these instructions (cf., e.g., Num 9:1ff.; 28:16ff.; Dt 16:1ff.). Deuteronomy 16:3 also emphasizes the haste of the act of setting forth in the midst of affliction: *"For seven days you shall eat unleavened bread with it — the bread of affliction — because you came out of the land of Egypt in great haste, so that all the days of your life you may remember the day of your departure from the land of Egypt."*

Lively remembrance of the affliction in Egypt, of the haste of setting forth on the way, of external danger! Remembrance of being preserved in this danger coming from outside, of being delivered out of this danger! These contents are of central significance for the Passover festival and the celebration of the Passover meal.[3]

3. The historical background of the Passover festival is suspected to be the following: originally a ritual of semi-nomads was carried out in the night before the annual change of

Holy communion also focuses human beings on suffering and danger. The Supper is related to the life, suffering, and death of Jesus Christ, in their many-layered significance for human beings. The Supper was instituted by Christ in the night in which he was handed over by his disciples and by God to the powers of this world. Here a decisive difference from the Passover meal commands our attention. The Passover meal remembers and celebrates a community bound in solidarity as it sets forth in a dangerous situation. By contrast, the Supper concentrates on a complex situation of danger not only from outside, but also from inside!

What is at issue is not only a personal threat to Jesus from his persecutors the high priests and from the Roman force of occupation. According to the testimony of the biblical traditions, Jesus is "handed over" to these powers. God himself does not hear Jesus' prayer: "My Father, if it is possible, let this cup pass from me; yet not what I want but what you want" (Mt 26:39; cf. Mk 14:36; Lk 22:42; Jn 12:27). Betrayal by his own disciples also threatens Jesus. This betrayal endangers not only Jesus' communion with his disciples, but also the communion of the disciples among themselves. In this process of "handing over," we must take with equal seriousness God's act of giving Jesus up to human beings and human beings' act of handing Jesus over to those who condemn and execute him. As the Gethsemane story makes particularly clear, there is an interplay here between God's act of giving Jesus up to the powers of the world and human beings' act of betraying Jesus. In the midst of being persecuted by

---

pasture from the wilderness to cultivated land. The blood of a sacrificial animal was supposed to ward off a ruinous demon. After Israel became a sedentary people, this custom was connected to the remembrance of the exodus from Egypt. In the late royal period the family and tribal festival became a festival in the state cult, celebrated in the Jerusalem temple (cf. 2 Chr 35). In the Exile, however, the family festival again gained importance, and after the reconstruction of the temple the family festival was also celebrated as a pilgrim festival. The Passover lamb was slaughtered in the temple and then consumed in the family group. See F. Thieberger, ed., *Jüdisches Fest — Jüdisches Brauch,* reprint (Berlin, 1976), pp. 198ff. I am grateful to Dennis Olson for pointing out that the sacrificial prescriptions for the Passover festival in Numbers 28 also provide for the sacrifice of a male goat "for a sin offering, to make atonement for you" (cf. Num 28:15, 30; 29:4, 11, 16, 19, 25). However, this sacrifice is also prescribed for other major festivals and for the monthly sacrifice "at the new moon" (cf. Num 28:15, 30; 29:4, 11, 16, 19, 25). It is therefore unlikely that there was an intentional transformation in the understanding of Passover. Nevertheless, here the idea that Israel also stands in need of internal renewal finds entrance into the rituals of the Passover festival.

the high priests, and of being handed over to the Roman force of occupation, looms the threat of betrayal by his own disciples.

To be sure, holy communion focuses particularly on Jesus' betrayal by Judas Iscariot.[4] But Jesus' sadness in view of the sleeping disciples on the Mount of Olives[5] and Peter's denial of Jesus[6] also stand directly in the context of the institution of the Supper! In these events the disciples' community with Jesus is threatened "from inside" with imminent dissolution. As such, these events fundamentally distinguish the Supper from the Passover meal, the nocturnal meal of setting forth on the way, of the divinely protected departure from a hostile environment upon which God visits destruction. The Supper is celebrated in view of the jeopardizing of community with Jesus not only from outside, but *also from inside.* Jesus is "handed over" even by "his own," even by the disciples. Here we must not overlook the fact that the disciples fall prey to a remarkable helplessness, and that they jeopardize themselves and their common life.

Holy communion recollects this situation of betrayal, of denial, of separation from God, and of the self-jeopardizing even of those who live in the most intimate communion with Jesus. Compared to the Passover festival, the danger and drama are heightened. This becomes clear particularly against the background that in the celebration of the Passover meal those who are persecuted stand in solidarity with one another in a community, setting forth united in its cause. By contrast, in Jesus' last meal the betrayer sits at the same table. The betrayer eats out of the same bowl with Jesus. Indeed, Jesus' hand and the hand of the betrayer dip together into the same bowl.[7] Reference to these facts makes clear the danger and the drama at Jesus' last meal, as does the tense and edgy question of Judas (Mt 23:25) and the disciples (Mk 14:19; Lk 22:23; cf. Jn 13:25): "Surely, not I?" Precisely in contrast to the solidarity characteristic of the community of the Exodus, recollected by the Passover meal, one can recognize in a drastic way what disintegration, what uncertainty, what mistrust, and what profound jeopardizing of the community appear here.

It is no secret that the Gospel according to John provides no holy communion texts comparable to those of the synoptic traditions. At the comparable position it reports Jesus' footwashing (Jn 13). But in John 6

4. Mk 14:10-11; Mt 26:14-16; Lk 22:3-6; cf. Jn 13.

5. Mk 14:26, 32-42; Mt 26:30, 36-46; Lk 22:39-46.

6. Mk 14:30-31, 53-54, 66-72; Mt 26:34-35, 57-58, 69-75; Lk 22:31-34, 54-62.

7. Cf. Lk 22:21; Mk 14:20; Mt 26:23; cf. Jn 13:26ff.

we find an announcement which is to be understood in terms of the theology of the Supper: "Unless you eat the flesh of the Human One and drink his blood, you have no life in you." Notably enough, this announcement also sparks strong disputes and splits among the disciples. It, too, is connected to a tension between the disciples and Jesus: "When many of his disciples heard it, they said, 'This teaching is difficult; who can accept it?' "[8]

Threats to Jesus, tensions, mistrust, edginess, sadness among the disciples, incipient or imminent dissolution of community: holy communion is celebrated and instituted as a "memorial meal" precisely in this context. This communal meal is instituted in the midst of great danger from without and within. It belongs to Jesus' characteristic forms for confronting aggression and violence.[9] (See the more detailed investigation of Jesus' words and meal actions in the next chapter, as well as in chapters 5 and 6.)

Was Jesus' Last Supper a Passover Meal or a Regular Jewish Meal?

Over and over, people have posed the question: When Jesus instituted the Supper, was he eating a normal Jewish meal with his disciples, or was he celebrating the Passover meal? In any case, before the report of Jesus' "last meal" with his disciples, the synoptic gospels speak of the preparation of the Passover meal (Mk 14:12ff.; Mt 26:17ff.). The longer Lukan text (Lk 22:15ff.) explicitly records Jesus' saying: "I have eagerly desired to eat this Passover with you before I suffer."

In his *Theological History of Early Christianity*,[10] Klaus Berger has presented the development of the early Christian Supper in a differentiated yet comprehensible manner. He comes to the conclusion that "on the ba-

8. Jn 6:60; cf. Jn 6:52. Luke follows the internal logic of the material when he places the dispute about rank among the disciples in the context of the story of the Supper (Lk 22:24ff.).

9. This sovereignty of the one who is threatened and suffering, but who recognizes and controls the aggressions directed against him, is characteristic of Jesus in various contexts. Cf. M. Welker, "Gewaltverzicht und Feindesliebe: Zu Matth 5,38-48," in J. Roloff and H. G. Ulrich, eds., *Einfach von Gott reden: Ein theologischer Diskurs,* Festschrift for Friedrich Mildenberger (Stuttgart: Kohlhammer, 1994), pp. 243-47.

10. Klaus Berger, *Theologiegeschichte des Urchristentums: Theologie des Neuen Testaments* (Tübingen: Francke, 1994), pp. 279ff.

sis of his communal life with the disciples, Jesus must have celebrated a last meal (at least *de facto*) at a particular point of time in his life. This was not a Passover meal, since Jesus would hardly have been crucified on the Passover festival, but rather . . . during the afternoon of the day before Passover." The majority of New Testament scholars today come to a similar judgment.

However, under the heading "The Last Supper — A Passover Meal!," Joachim Jeremias in his famous book *The Eucharistic Words of Jesus*[11] gave a list of reasons why Jesus' last meal was indeed a Passover meal. The most striking of his arguments are:

1. According to Mark 14:17; Matthew 26:20, and also according to 1 Corinthians 11:23 and John 13:30, Jesus' last meal was held "when it was evening" or at night. Apart from Matthew 14:15, where the feeding of the five thousand explicitly takes place after the mealtime had already passed by, a normal meal was never held at a nighttime hour. Only festival meals could stretch into the night. But "from its inception the passover meal was eaten at night."[12]

2. The synoptic writers are in agreement (Mk 14:18; Mt 26:20; Lk 22:14; but also Jn 13:12, 23, 25, 28) that Jesus reclined at table with his disciples at the last meal. This, too, by no means follows as a matter of course. According to Jeremias, it can be explained only on the basis of the ritual form of the Passover meal.[13]

3. According to Mark 14:18-22 and Matthew 26:21-26, Jesus breaks bread only in the course of the meal. According to Jeremias, "that is remarkable, because the ordinary meals began with the breaking of bread." By contrast, one of the children's questions that introduce the Passover devotion is: "How is it that on every other evening we dip bread into the dish but on this evening we simply dip (without bread) into the dish?" Jeremias gives the following commentary: "This children's question shows conclusively that the passover meal was the only family meal in the year at which the serving of a dish (Mk 14.20) preceded the breaking of bread (Mk 14.22)."[14]

4. Finally, along with some other perspectives that argue for a Passover

11. Joachim Jeremias, *The Eucharistic Words of Jesus,* trans. Norman Perrin, The New Testament Library (London: SCM, 1966), pp. 41ff.

12. Jeremias, *The Eucharistic Words of Jesus,* p. 46.

13. Jeremias, *The Eucharistic Words of Jesus,* pp. 48-49.

14. Jeremias, *The Eucharistic Words of Jesus,* pp. 49-50.

meal, Jeremias claims that the words with which Jesus gives the bread and wine, and his — as Jeremias says — "altogether extraordinary manner of announcing his passion," can only be explained by the fact that Jesus picked up and transformed the established interpretation of the particular elements of the meal in the Passover ritual. "The ritual interpretation of the special elements of the passover meal which we have described was the occasion for the interpretation which Jesus gave to the bread and the wine at the Last Supper. That means: structurally Jesus modelled his sayings upon the ritual of interpreting the passover."[15]

However, Jeremias also presents a list of counterarguments. Among these the point mentioned above, that the time of crucifixion had to have been *before* the Passover festival, is especially weighty. In their book *The Historical Jesus,* Gerd Theissen and Annette Merz have summarized the "criticism of the interpretation of the last meal as a Passover meal":[16]

a. The early Christians celebrated the Supper frequently, while Passover is celebrated annually.
b. The Passover meal is a familial celebration, while at Jesus' meal the "the women who followed him to Jerusalem are not present."
c. John and Paul support a chronology according to which "Jesus died on Friday, 14 Nisan, before the beginning of the feast of the Passover (at sundown)."
d. Most importantly, Theissen and Merz name a multitude of indices from the (pre-)Markan passion story which point to Jesus' condemnation and death before the Passover festival. For example:

  - Mark 14:1-2: It was the will of Jesus' opponents that he die before the festival;
  - Mark 15:6: The Passover amnesty for Barabbas;
  - Mark 15:42: The dating of the crucifixion on a "day of preparation": i.e., the day before the Sabbath;
  - Mark 15:46: Joseph of Arimathea bought a linen cloth in order to bury Jesus, which would hardly have been possible on the Sabbath.

15. Jeremias, *The Eucharistic Words of Jesus,* pp. 56, 60-61. Cf. Peter Stuhlmacher, "Das neutestamentliche Zeugnis vom Herrenmahl," in P. Stuhlmacher, *Jesus von Nazareth — Christus des Glaubens* (Stuttgart: Calwer, 1988), pp. 70ff.

16. Gerd Theissen and Annette Merz, *The Historical Jesus: A Comprehensive Guide* (Minneapolis: Fortress, 1998), pp. 426-27.

At the core, the whole discussion of the New Testament scholars preserves the tension that on the one hand, the longer Lukan text (Lk 22:14-20) "clearly takes its orientation from the flow of a Passover meal," while on the other hand, the text with clearly the earliest historical origin, 1 Corinthians 11:23b-25, "evinces no reference to a Passover meal."[17] What does this mean for the question "What happens in holy communion?"

How Often Should We Celebrate the Supper?

We should thus reckon with the fact that *two traditions* are to be found in the New Testament material, and that they were bound together in a relationship of tension:

- The one tradition connects Jesus' Supper with the Jewish Passover.
- The other tradition distinguishes between the two, and takes its orientation from a normal Jewish meal.

This tension, though, is completely appropriate! On the one hand, there is a continuity between the Passover meal and the Supper, insofar as both cases institute "a memorial" of God's decisive action of deliverance toward and among human beings. On the other hand, we must pay attention to the difference: Holy communion celebrates deliverance not only from an "outside" threat, but also from an "inside" danger, including self-imposed danger.

It is obvious that the early church clearly perceived the difference between the Supper and the Passover festival. Nothing argues for the Supper having been celebrated, like Passover, only once per year! What can appear vexatious for historical reconstruction ("Now, did Jesus celebrate the last meal with his disciples as a Passover meal or not? Yes or no?!") is systematically and practically fruitful precisely in its undecidability. If Jesus did celebrate a Passover meal here, he in any case transformed it. The concentration is no longer primarily on the exodus from an external threat and on the slaughter of the Passover lamb. Now the central place is occu-

17. Otfried Hofius, "Herrenmahl und Herrenmahlsparadosis: Erwägungen zu 1 Kor 11,23b-25," in *Paulusstudien,* 2nd ed., WUNT 51 (Tübingen: Mohr, 1994), pp. 203-40, 211; Hofius, "'Für euch gegeben zur Vergebung der Sünden': Vom Sinn des Heiligen Abendmahls," *Zeitschrift für Theologie und Kirche* 95 (1998): 320.

pied by the community's self-imposed danger and self-destruction — in addition to the external threat — and by Jesus' readiness to give his body and blood for "his own." However, if Jesus celebrated his last meal with his disciples not as a Passover meal, but "only" as a normal Jewish meal, since he would already "have been crucified during the afternoon of the day before Passover," in multiple ways this meal still points backwards and forwards toward the Passover festival.

This double orientation is important for the way in which Christians and Jews are bound together while at the same time having different traditions. The custom in some Christian communities of annually celebrating a "Seder-communion" (on Maundy Thursday, for instance) takes account of this fact. This celebration, which appropriates both the Old Testament Passover tradition and the New Testament Supper tradition, can make clear the continuity between the Jewish and the Christian "memorial meal" without confusing the Passover festival and holy communion.

The double orientation is also helpful in answering the question "How often should we celebrate holy communion?" Of course, it does not prescribe any simple answer or any rigid rhythm. Instead it establishes two polar values: at the one extreme, annually (Passover) — at the other extreme, daily (Jewish meal)! This double boundary by no means leads to arbitrariness, if we really observe the double orientation and the rhythm jointly shared in principle by both the annual festival and the daily meal. From this perspective, the monthly or weekly celebration that has established itself in most congregations makes good sense.

Daily celebration threatens to devalue the significance of the Supper. Its celebration should not become routine. For several reasons it must not in any case lose its festival and symbolic character. Therefore it makes sense to pay attention to the opposite polar value: only once per year! Yet the solely annual celebration of the Supper — which is the custom in some congregations — carries its own dangers. A merely annual celebration can hardly give free course to the significance and influence of the Supper in the life of the church and of believers. Holy communion threatens to become a disconnected rarity.[18] That does grave damage because, as a rule, we clearly recognize an external threat to the community, we clearly long for deliverance from the external

18. Cf. J. Fangmeier, "Karl Barth und das Heilige Abendmahl: Ein Hinweis," *Reformierte Kirchenzeitung* 140 (1999): 14.

threat, and we gratefully celebrate the deliverance when it occurs. By contrast, an internal threat to a human community is more cunning. Sometimes we do not even perceive it. We have grown acccustomed to it; we have adjusted to it. When someone points it out, we contest it, we "explain it away." At other times, it appears as a catastrophe, a destiny against which we cannot in any case do anything. We accept it in a torpor of suffering or despair.

By contrast, holy communion cultivates sensitivity to the powerful ways in which this world jeopardizes itself — powers from which the churches are by no means free! It cultivates sensitivity to the powers of "the night of betrayal," which the Bible calls "sin" (cf. esp. chapters 6 and 10). In order not to lose this sensitivity, but above all in order to preserve the vitality of joy over God's liberating and creative action among human beings, we should celebrate the Supper much more often than once per year.

Results

The Supper stands in material continuity with the Jewish Passover meal. Like the Passover meal, the Supper serves the vital recollection of divine preservation in great danger and of deliverance from this danger.

However, the Supper is fundamentally different from the Passover meal, in that the Supper celebrates not only the experience of setting forth and departing from a hostile environment on which God visits destruction. The Supper makes clear that Jesus' community is jeopardized not only "from outside," but also "from inside" — even by his disciples. Judas' betrayal, the disciples asleep in Gethsemane, and Peter's denial make this clear. In the situation of external and internal danger, Jesus institutes the "memorial meal" of liberation.

It is important to recognize this in order to understand the connection between holy communion and liberation from the power of sin (cf. esp. chapters 6 and 10), and in order to prevent the celebration of the Supper from being misused for the purposes of moralism and church law (cf. chapters 4 and 10).

The question "Was Jesus' last meal a Passover meal or a normal Jewish meal?" cannot be given a definitive historical answer. It establishes two polar values for our orientation in deciding how often we should celebrate the Supper.

- In no case should we celebrate holy communion less often than once per year (Passover). Rather, taking note of the second polar value, we should celebrate it with more frequent regularity.
- In no case should we celebrate holy communion more frequently than once per day (normal Jewish meal). Rather, taking note of the first polar value, we should celebrate it considerably less frequently.

The connection of two traditions makes possible in this tension a creative freedom. With the decision to celebrate the Supper weekly or monthly, many churches have made sensible use of this freedom.

CHAPTER 3

". . . He Took Bread, Gave Thanks, Broke It, and Gave It to Them Saying: Take and Eat . . ."

We Must Not Separate the Glorification of God from the Mutual Acceptance of Human Beings

The third answer to the question "What happens in holy communion?" is: *Holy communion cannot be understood without the symbolic action with which the meal is celebrated. In this symbolic action God is gratefully glorified and human beings accept and welcome one another.*

Theological texts and ecumenical pronouncements about the Supper repeatedly cite a text from the second century which became very influential in both the East and West. It comes from Justin Martyr, *Apology,* 1.66: "Jesus took the bread, gave thanks, and said: 'Do this in remembrance of me: This is my body . . .'"

It is noteworthy that from early on theologians have concentrated particularly on "the thanksgiving" in the Supper, and as a consequence have said that the Supper is a thanksgiving, a "eucharist." It is indeed a fact that thanksgiving to God the creator and thankful remembrance of Jesus Christ and his salvific activity stand at the very center of the Supper. Yet this thanksgiving is tied to the symbolic celebration of the meal. The one-sided emphasis on the "thanksgiving" pushes to the sidelines or treats as merely an attendant implication that set of actions which the biblical texts highlight in almost verbose detail:

- taking the bread,
- breaking the bread after giving thanks,

- distributing or giving the bread,
- inviting the recipients to take and eat the broken bread.

In like manner, the one-sided emphasis on the thanksgiving obscures the whole differentiated action in connection with the cup.[1]

Why the Supper Is More Than a Thanksgiving, a "Eucharist"

Obscuring the differentiated nexus of actions involving the taking and giving of bread and wine has fateful consequences for the understanding of holy communion. Perhaps at first glance this nexus of actions does not appear to be anything special. Yet there are good reasons why the biblical texts present it in such detail. Obscuring this differentiated action has fateful consequences because we lose sight of the particularities of the thanksgiving in the Supper in comparison with other ways of thanking God. There are many possibilities for thanking God the creator or the triune God both inside and outside the worship service. There are also many ways to "remember Christ" with thanksgiving. Finally, there are several possibilities for connecting thanksgiving to God and the "memory of Christ." However, among the many possible ways — which have in part taken on liturgical forms — of giving thanks to God and of calling Christ and his salvific activity to remembrance, the Supper is highlighted in a particular way. A symbolic nexus of actions immediately connects thanksgiving to God and the "remembrance of Christ": They are connected by virtue of the fact that bread is taken, broken, distributed, received, and eaten, and by virtue of an analogous process with the cup and wine. We must not tear apart a fundamental relationship of human beings to God (in thanks and remembrance) and a fundamental relationship between human beings (in the symbolic celebration of the meal). Jesus gives thanks not simply for the gifts which he then consumes. He gives thanks for the gifts which he gives to others, which he shares.

According to Justin, Paul's statement in 1 Corinthians 10:16b — "The bread that we break, is it not a sharing in the body of Christ?" —

1. In his famous book *The Shape of the Liturgy* (2nd ed. [London: Dacre, 1945]), D. G. Dix took this differentiated set of actions as his point of departure in striving after a renewal of the practice and piety of the Supper. See also D. J. Kennedy and D. Mann, *Making the Eucharistic Prayer Work* (Nottingham: Grove Books, 1988).

would have to read: "The bread over which we say thanks, is it not a sharing in the body of Christ?" If we want to recognize what happens in holy communion, we must neither neglect the thanksgiving and the remembrance of Christ (the *anamnesis*), nor undervalue or even ignore the richly articulated nexus of symbolic actions happening in the Supper that are concentrated on the bread and wine, and on the communal meal and the meal community. In this regard the ecumenical dialogues between the Anglicans and Roman Catholics can make important contributions to overcoming a reductionist and distorted understanding of the Supper.[2]

The Anglicans and Roman Catholics observe that "in the course of the Church's history several traditions have developed in expressing Christian understanding of the eucharist. (For example, various names have become customary as descriptions of the eucharist: Lord's Supper, liturgy, holy mysteries, synaxis, mass, holy communion. The eucharist has become the most universally accepted term.)"[3] The dialogues between Anglicans and Roman Catholics emphasize the great richness of the process that is summarized with the term "eucharist": "Christ is present and active, in various ways, in the entire eucharistic celebration. It is the same Lord who through the proclaimed word invites his people to his table, who through his minister presides at that table, and who gives himself sacramentally in the body and blood of his paschal sacrifice."[4] In order not to obscure this richness of Christ's act of making himself present (see especially chapter 5), we must in no case separate the thanksgiving from the action of sacramental eating and drinking. This means that the predominance of the designation "eucharist," "thanksgiving," must not suppress either the symbolic meal or the multiformity of Christ's presence in the Supper!

More than a few times in recent years Lutherans and Reformed have proposed an unhesitating use of the term "eucharist" — which is the most widely accepted designation — in order to move beyond "mass" and "Lord's Supper" to find an expression equally acceptable to Protestants

2. See esp. the "Windsor Statement" (1971) of the Anglican–Roman Catholic International Commission, and "Eucharistic Doctrine: Elucidation" (1979), which was elaborated in part on the basis of reactions to the "Windsor Statement."

3. "Windsor Statement" 1971 [A-RC], p. 69.

4. "Windsor Statement," pp. 70-71; cf. "Eucharistic Doctrine: Elucidation" 1979 [A-RC], pp. 74-75.

and Catholics.[5] This proposal has been accompanied by the lament that many Protestants regard talk of the "eucharist" as a "Trojan horse" that will "smuggle in unreformed ideas about the sacrament."[6] One of the ways in which the proposal to regard and to employ the expression "eucharist" as a designation that overarches the confessional positions has been grounded is to assert that Calvin himself observed that the sacrifice of thanksgiving, "which we have called eucharistic . . . is indispensable in the Supper."[7]

Yet we must not in the process suppress the problem of reducing the Supper to "the thanksgiving." It is in fact a huge leap from the correct insight that the thanksgiving, the eucharist, is indispensable to the Supper, to the recommendation that we make the term "eucharist" the primary designation of the entire event of the Supper. In the past this designation has been able to go hand in hand with a neglect or even an elision of the differentiated ritual process of celebrating the meal — and it can still happen today. As accurate as it is to note that the expression "eucharist" has enjoyed particular ecumenical success in recent years, it remains equally important not to be over hasty in removing from circulation designations that, even if they are not materially more appropriate, are at least complementary. Of particular note in this regard are the designation "Lord's Supper," coined on the basis of 1 Corinthians 11:20, and the simple designation "Supper," recalling the context in which the meal was instituted.

In the Supper the prayer of thanksgiving, the eucharist, is inseparably bound to the breaking, distributing, taking, and eating of the bread and the drinking of the wine. This means that in the Supper the thanksgiving to God the creator is in itself only an epistemic or linguistic act. Nor is it exhausted by liturgical expression, in prayer and praise. It is bound up, however symbolically, with a communal meal in which the participants share bread and wine with one another, and in which all participants take equal part. What happens here is a process of symbolic, reciprocal welcome and acceptance among human beings. Social connectedness, basic responsibility, and basic trust find symbolic expression. In a communal

5. Cf. Alasdair I. C. Heron, *Table and Tradition: Toward an Ecumenical Understanding of the Eucharist* (Philadelphia: Westminster, 1983), p. xiii.

6. Heron, *Table and Tradition,* p. xiii.

7. "It is no very great jump from Calvin to restore the word itself [eucharist] as an alternative to 'Supper'" (Heron, *Table and Tradition,* p. xiii, with reference to John Calvin, *Institutes of the Christian Religion,* IV, XVIII, 16-17).

meal all participants make sure that all the other participants get enough to eat. There is a way in which there is no better way of symbolizing basic justice among humans than the communal meal. The symbolic celebration of the Supper makes this clear by virtue of the fact that everyone who shares in the celebration receives a piece of bread and a drink of wine.

We must not by any means obscure this basic process of the symbolic formation of community in the act of sharing and distributing! It is this basic process to which the thanksgiving, the eucharist, looks forward — although not only to it! — and it itself refers back to the thanksgiving.

"When the Word Comes to the Element, There Is a Sacrament": A Deficiency Even in Augustine and Luther?

By means of a problematic — often highly speculative — concentration on "the elements" of bread and wine, Protestant theology, too, has contributed to the neglect of both the symbolic process of taking, sharing, and giving, and the invitation to take, eat, and drink. The precise investigation of the symbolic nexus of actions in the Supper was supplanted by speculations concerning the connection between "the elements" and, on the one hand, "the word," and, on the other hand, a suprasensible reality.

In terms of the history of theology, the biggest effect was exercised by Augustine's famous statement, "When the word comes to the element, there is a sacrament."[8] Luther picked up this statement and claimed: "This saying of St. Augustine is so accurate and well put that it is doubtful if he has said anything better."[9] In spite of the overwhelming united

8. A. Augustinus, *In Iohannis Evangelium Tractatus* LXXX, 3, Corpus Christianorum, Series Latina 36, p. 529. Concerning the conceptual history of the word "sacrament," see William A. Van Roo, *The Christian Sacrament* (Rome, 1992). For sacramental doctrine in the Reformation tradition, see Alfons Skowronek, *Sakrament in der evangelischen Theologie der Gegenwart: Haupttypen der Sakramentsauffassungen in der zeitgenössischen, vorwiegend deutschen evangelischen Theologie* (Paderborn: Schöningh, 1971). For sacramental doctrine in the Catholic tradition, see Alexandre Ganoczy, *Einführung in die katholische Sakramentenlehre* (Darmstadt: Wissenschaftliche Buchgesellschaft, 1979). Cf. also Michael G. Lawler, *Symbol and Sacrament: A Contemporary Sacramental Theology* (New York: Paulist, 1987), pp. 29ff.

9. Martin Luther, "The Large Catechism," in Theodore G. Tappert, trans. and ed., *The Book of Concord: The Confessions of the Evangelical Lutheran Church* (Philadelphia: Fortress, 1959), p. 448.

authority of Augustine and Luther we must voice reservations about this impressive "saying." Just as the sacrament of the Supper is not only a thanksgiving to God, so it is equally true that it is not just a "coming together" of word and element. It is essential to focus clearly and explicitly not just on the thanksgiving, but on the articulated symbolic and ritual process of taking bread, breaking, giving, taking, and eating, as well as on the corresponding actions with the wine and cup, in the gathered community. It is essential to do this if we are to gain an appropriate perception of the process of the Supper, including of "the elements."

Of course, this articulated process is indissolubly connected to the words of the Supper's institution, and to the thanksgiving. But without the articulated *symbolic action* of breaking bread, of sharing, of inviting to take and eat, of giving and taking, and of actually eating, no "sacrament of the Supper" comes out of either the thanksgiving or the connection of "word and element," however that connection might be understood. By not regarding the complex symbolic action that is carried out in the table community's celebration of the meal, we run the danger of hatching and sending out into the world all sorts of chimerical conceptions and magical notions of the connection between "word and element."

The joint declarations of Anglicans and Roman Catholics on the global level clarify very nicely the transition from the traditional understanding, centered on the eucharist, to the broadened and deepened understanding, which takes account of the entire process of the Supper. At first glance the traditional understanding seems to hold the upper hand. The "Windsor Statement" of 1971 explicitly says: "According to the traditional order of the liturgy the consecratory prayer *(anaphora)* leads to the communion of the faithful. Through this prayer of thanksgiving, a word of faith addressed to the Father, the bread and wine become the body and blood of Christ by the action of the Holy Spirit, so that in communion we eat the flesh of Christ and drink his blood." But at the same time the text emphasizes that "the Lord's words at the last supper, 'Take and eat; this is my body,' do not allow us to dissociate the gift of the presence and the act of sacramental eating."[10]

Moreover, the Salisbury "Elucidation" of 1979 rejects in manifold ways a physicalist (and correspondingly magical) misunderstanding of the "change" of the elements. The discussion of transubstantiation culminates in the statement that "the community, the Body of Christ, by par-

10. "Windsor Statement" 1971 [A-RC], p. 71.

taking of the sacramental body of the risen Lord, grows into the unity God intends for his church." The point of transubstantiation is the "ultimate change intended by God . . . the transformation of human beings into the likeness of Christ."[11]

The Salisbury "Elucidation" is similarly subtle in its treatment of Roman Catholic tabernacle piety (see also chapter 1). Discussing the reservation of the elements, it cautiously observes that "differences arise between those who would practise reservation for this reason only [i.e., distribution to those who cannot be present at the eucharistic celebration], and those who would also regard it as a means of eucharistic devotion." With regard to these different forms of piety, the document repeatedly emphasizes that dissociating the veneration of the consecrated elements from the celebration of the Supper in the gathered community contradicts "the true doctrine of the eucharist."[12] These statements pull the rug out from under a piety and a theological practice that fix their concentration on "the elements" independently of the action of sacramental eating and drinking. The words of institution, of thanksgiving, and of remembrance, the elements of bread and wine, and the symbolic action, the symbolic celebration of the meal, belong indissolubly together in the Supper. Only the interconnection of word, element, and symbolic action of the gathered community constitutes the sacrament.

Why the Supper Is More Than a Ritual of Mutual Acceptance and Symbolic Righteousness

The meal symbolizes mutual acceptance and a basic will for justice. It expresses reconciliation among human beings. As important as it is to emphasize this aspect over against "eucharistic" forms that threaten to suppress it, it would be just as bad to jump from the frying pan into the fire. It would be dangerous to have a "cult of the (self-)righteous community," appealing to the symbolic communal meal for support. It would be a fateful development if the Supper became a demonstrative self-presentation of the supposedly righteous meal community. Even the ritual self-presentation of a community which took the obligation of mutual accep-

11. "Eucharistic Doctrine: Elucidation" 1979 [A-RC], p. 75; cf. "Final Report" 1981 [A-RC], p. 65.

12. "Eucharistic Doctrine: Elucidation" 1979 [A-RC], p. 76.

tance and basic justice with the greatest seriousness — or at least wanted to do so — would obscure and betray that which happens in holy communion. Such a self-presentation would have understood nothing of the seriousness of the "night of betrayal," of Christ's self-giving, and of God's creative action toward human beings in the Supper.

Holy communion is by no means simply about the symbolization of just, brotherly and sisterly relations. If we want to understand what happens in holy communion, thanksgiving to God, the glorification of God, and the breaking and distribution of bread and wine must not be torn asunder and placed over against each other. We must not combat or replace the "eucharistic" one-sidedness with the one-sidedness of a "meal of peace." Theologians are quick to distinguish between the "vertical dimension" (the relation of God to humans or of humans to God) and the "horizontal dimension" (the relation of humans among themselves). In the Supper the relation of humans to God and the intrahuman relations, the "vertical" and "horizontal" dimensions, must remain closely and indissolubly bound together![13] The differentiated symbolic process — "He took the bread, gave thanks to God, broke the bread, gave it to his disciples, and said: 'Take and eat . . .'" — calls attention to that fact.

Jesus' Meals and the Glorification of the Creator

Joachim Jeremias has rightly insisted:

> The wrong way to develop an understanding of the last supper is to begin from the words of interpretation, because in this way the so-called "founding meal" is isolated. Indeed, it ought really to be said that this isolation of the last supper through the centuries has made it very difficult to recognize its . . . significance. In reality, the "founding meal" is only one link in a long chain of meals which Jesus shared with his followers and which they continued after Easter. These gatherings at table, which provoked such scandal because Jesus excluded

13. See Martin Luther, "The Blessed Sacrament of the Holy and True Body of Christ, and the Brotherhoods," trans. Jeremiah J. Schindel, rev. E. Theodore Bachmann, in Helmut T. Lehmann and Jaroslav Pelikan, eds., *Luther's Works,* American Edition, vol. 35, *Word and Sacrament I,* ed. E. Theodore Bachmann (Philadelphia: Muhlenberg, 1960), pp. 45ff.

no one from them, even open sinners, and which thus expressed the heart of his message, were types of the feast to come in the time of salvation. . . . The last supper has its historical roots in this chain of gatherings.[14]

One of the difficulties in recognizing the inner dynamic and the interconnection of the parts of the Supper consists in the fact that the actual wording of Jesus' prayer of thanksgiving and blessing has not been transmitted to us. The Greek text uses the verbs *eucharisteo* and *eulogeo* for the prayer of thanksgiving and blessing. We can at any rate translate *eucharisteo* as "give thanks" or "gratefully praise." Matthew and Mark use it for the cup, and 1 Corinthians 11 also uses it for the bread. Its use indicates a prayer of thanksgiving, a grateful glorification of God. By contrast, with regard to the bread Mark and Matthew speak of *eulogeo* — "praise, bless" — and 1 Corinthians 10 calls the meal's cup the "cup of blessing." It seems likely that both expressions are used without substantive difference, although *eulogeo* ("praise, bless, call down God's gracious power") evinces a stronger basic feature of "glorification" than does the "thanksgiving." But how do the glorification of God and the distribution of the bread hang together?

Observations concerning what happens in the normal Jewish meal can at least start us thinking here.[15] The actual meal begins with the "word over the bread": "Blessed are you, O Lord our God, Sovereign of all worlds, who brings forth bread from the earth!" Then the bread is broken into pieces, given to each person present, and the meal begins.

What is initially striking is that God's blessing is not being beseeched, but rather God is being blessed. Evidently in Jewish understanding this does not conflict with the "right relation" between God and human beings, since God is, after all, explicitly called the "Lord our God, Sovereign of all worlds." The second striking element is that God is not thanked for bringing forth grain from the earth, but for bringing forth bread.

Taken together, both aspects indicate that the "thanksgiving to the Cre-

14. Joachim Jeremias, *New Testament Theology,* vol. 1, *The Proclamation of Jesus,* trans. John Bowden, The New Testament Library (London: SCM, 1971), pp. 289-90. Cf. Gerd Theissen, "Soziale Integration und sakramentales Handeln: Eine Analyse von 1 Kor 11,11-34," *Novum Testamentum* 16 (1974): 179-206.

15. I take my orientation from Klaus Berger, *Manna, Mehl und Sauerteig: Korn und Mehl im Alltag der frühen Christen* (Stuttgart: Quell, 1993), pp. 128ff.

ator over the bread" is more than merely the recognition of creatures' "absolute dependence" — an absolute dependence on that which is brought forth from nature by God's will and God's goodness. The cultural activity of human beings, which turns grain into bread, and the thanksgiving that this activity is possible, are thus incorporated into the thanksgiving to the Creator. Moreover, the human act of giving thanks and glory to God can go as far as "blessing God." This has a strange sound to it, although we also find corresponding expressions in individual psalms. We can still pretty well imagine what it means to beseech God's blessing, or even to bless a fellow human or a piece of bread, and thereby to call down God's gracious power on a person or a means of nourishment. But to bless God — what is that supposed to mean? Is God interested in being blessed by humans?

Beyond all Christian anxieties about confusing God and humanity, and about a "collaboration" between God and human beings that concedes too much power to human beings, what we have here is evidently the perception of a state of affairs that is also addressed by the biblical creation accounts. To a certain extent, human beings are destined to take part in God's creative action! According to Genesis 1, this authorization has to do primarily with dominion over the animals; according to Genesis 2, primarily with the "tilling and keeping" of vegetation.[16] Without the participation of human beings a cultivated world and fruitful vegetation capable of regenerating itself are biblically unthinkable. Nature and culture are reciprocally interconnected.

It is important that we see God's interest in being given the thanks, the glorification, indeed the blessing of human beings, and that we see God's will to have humans participate in making it possible for bread to be brought forth from the earth. When we see these things, the connection between God's creative activity and God's interest in human justice, in our mutual acceptance, and in reconciliation and peace becomes very clear! Justice and mutual acceptance on the part of human beings are indispensable in order for humans to follow their creaturely destiny and for God's intentions to achieve the goal of (1) "bringing forth bread from the earth" with the help of human beings and (2) receiving thanks and glory from humans.[17]

16. Cf. Welker, *Creation and Reality*, trans. John F. Hoffmeyer (Minneapolis: Fortress, 1999), pp. 60ff. For bibliography, see pp. 95-98.

17. See Patrick D. Miller, *They Cried to the Lord: The Form and Theology of Biblical Prayer* (Minneapolis: Fortress, 1994), pp. 179ff.

On the contrary, if injustice and the absence of peace rule among humans and endanger humans themselves, that is a tremendous force in opposition to God's intentions. Thanking God and praising God are indissolubly connected with God's will for justice and for human beings' mutual acceptance. Joy in God and peace among humans cannot be separated. "Eucharist" and the symbolic meal of justice and mutual acceptance must not be torn asunder.

A church ordinance written in Syria between A.D. 100 and 130, and cited in numerous liturgies of holy communion, says: "As this broken bread was scattered over the hills and then, when gathered, became one mass, so may Thy Church be gathered from the ends of the earth into Thy Kingdom."[18] In light of the above insights we must add: Without the community defined by God's will for justice and for mutual acceptance, the "bread scattered over the hills" cannot be gathered together and cannot nourish the community. But in the context of the "night of betrayal," this will for justice and for mutual acceptance is by no means self-evident! Along with the bread "from the earth" that nourishes human beings, we also need a bread which various biblical traditions call "bread from heaven." This bread is needed in order to bring to reality God's creative intentions even among hostile human beings and in a threatened and self-jeopardizing world. God's far-reaching, creative care is needed in order to make sure that bread can be brought forth from the earth and that God can be praised and blessed as "Sovereign of all worlds."

If the activity of Jesus Christ establishes this reconciled communion of human beings both with God and with each other, we can understand why the most diverse biblical traditions connect Christ and his work to the "beginning of creation" and the "foundation of creation." The Supper concretizes this experience of the "foundation of creation," inasmuch as human beings come together in the praise of God, in the explicit will for justice, in mutual acceptance, and in peace.

On the basis of these insights we can give a clear answer to a question that is asked over and over again concerning the "elements" of bread and wine: Can we celebrate the Supper only with these elements? Or can we use, for instance, milk and honey or apples and water?

18. "The Didache, or the Teaching of the Twelve Apostles," in *Ancient Christian Writers: The Works of the Fathers in Translation,* vol. 6, trans. and annot. James A. Kleist (Westminster, Md.: Newman, 1961), p. 20.

Bread and Wine as "Gifts of Creation": Can They Be Replaced by Other "Elements"?

As "gifts of creation," bread and wine are not simple "gifts of nature." This means that there is no bread and wine without the successful communion of human beings with each other and with nature. This comes to expression in seed-time and harvest, and in the processes that produce bread as a daily means of nourishment and wine as a festive drink. But without the creative activity of God's Spirit, there is no intrahuman community and no successful community of humans and nature. Without these far-reaching interconnections bread and wine cannot be brought forth as "gifts of creation." Their presence points to the prior presence of a beneficent order, for which we cannot thank God enough.

It is only in this context that we can perceive the meaning of bread and wine, the so-called "elements." Bread and wine do not stand for just any nourishment or just any drink. Instead bread and wine are gifts that have been acquired in the creative interaction of God, human beings, and other creatures and creaturely realms. It is by no means self-evident that human beings fulfill their role in this process. After all, by our injustice, unmercifulness, and manifold betrayal of communion with God and with each other, we threaten to abandon — to fall out of — the relation to God the creator and to our creaturely destiny.

The "gifts of creation," which owe their existence to the divinely intended interplay of nature and the cultivating and cultural activities of humans, cannot be replaced by fruits and water or by other pure gifts of nature. As gifts of creation, bread stands for the basic means of nourishment, and wine stands for the festive drink. Moreover, bread can be torn, broken, and divided, and wine permits the association with blood (aspects whose significance will emerge in chapters 5ff.). We thus have a clear "rule of translation" for the correct choice of elements for the Supper in various cultures.

If other cultures have other basic means of nourishment and other festive drinks than bread and wine, if they are gifts of creation in the sense described above (i.e., they owe their existence to the interaction of nature and culture), and if they permit the association with the torn body and the blood, these means of nourishment should be used in the Supper as "elements." Where this "translation" is not possible, where the basic means of nourishment and the festive drink do not allow the incorporation of these meanings (tearable or breakable), bread and wine should be used — with occasional explanations.

This does not yet answer the so-called grape juice question that has become acutely pressing in recent years in many Christian communities. Can or should the Supper be regularly or at least occasionally celebrated with grape juice instead of with wine — for example, out of regard for persons suffering from alcoholism? This question cannot be answered on the basis of the insights acquired up to this point. We still need further clarification of what happens in holy communion (see chapter 4).

Results

The thanksgiving, the "eucharist," is an essential aspect of the Supper. Thanksgiving to God the creator and thankful remembrance of Christ and his self-giving are central to this celebration.

Yet along with the thanksgiving, there is a second center: the communal taking, breaking, and distributing of the bread, and the corresponding symbolic action with the cup and wine. The action in connection with the bread and wine expresses human beings' welcome and acceptance of each other. The language of "eucharist" does not express with sufficient clarity the significance of this process of symbolic actions.

The theological concentration on the interconnection of "word and element" can also lead to the neglect of the symbolic action. Augustine's familiar formula: "When the word comes to the element, there is a sacrament," is in need of corrective supplementation: word, element, and symbolic action constitute the sacrament.

However, it is just as unacceptable to isolate the symbolic action. Holy communion is by no means simply a celebration of good intrahuman relations or a ritual that obligates the participants to engage in good social behavior. Against the background of the "night of betrayal," the Supper celebrates both reconciliation with God and reconciliation among human beings. Reconciliation with God is particularly celebrated in thanksgiving and glorification; reconciliation among humans is particularly celebrated in the symbolic meal. Both aspects are equally necessary in order to glorify God the creator in word and deed.

On this basis it is also possible rightly to understand "the elements" of bread and wine as "gifts of creation." Bread as a basic means of nourishment and wine as a festive drink are not mere "gifts of nature." They owe their existence to the creative interaction of nature, on the one hand, and of human cultivating and cultural activities, on the other hand. Only a basic means of nourishment and a festive drink which are gifts of creation in this sense, and which are capable of representing Christ's body and blood (see chapters 5ff.) can take the place of bread and wine in other times and cultures.

CHAPTER 4

"Whoever, Therefore, Eats the Bread or Drinks the Cup of the Lord in an Unworthy Manner . . ."

If God Accepts Human Beings Unconditionally, Even the Community's Enemies . . . How Can Misuse of the Meal Be Prevented?

What happens in holy communion? The fourth answer is: *Holy communion is an event of unconditional acceptance of all the participants.* All who — in whatever way — deny this or mask it by the way in which they celebrate the meal, are celebrating the meal "unworthily."

What Is the Meaning of the Oppressive References to "Unworthy Eating and Drinking" and to Coming Together "Unto Judgment"?

While many religious and liturgical forms clearly permit human beings to participate even if they do not agree in their understanding of what they are doing, the Supper seems petty in this regard. After all, Paul repeatedly says that the gathering for the Supper can occur "unto judgment" (1 Cor 11:34). More precisely:

1 Corinthians 11:27-29, 31-32:

27 Whoever, therefore, eats the bread or drinks the cup of the Lord in an unworthy manner will be answerable for the body and blood of the Lord.

28 Examine youselves, and only then eat of the bread and drink of the cup.
29 For all who eat and drink without discerning the body, eat and drink judgment against themselves. . . .
31 But if we judged ourselves, we would not be judged.
32 But when we are judged by the Lord, we are disciplined so that we may not be condemned along with the world.

How, though, are we supposed to "examine" ourselves, how are we supposed to know whether we are eating "unworthily," whether we are coming together "unto judgment," if it is not clear what is happening in holy communion? This has repeatedly been the spot at which a diffuse moral and religious sensibility has been propagated among the laity, and a more or less rigid readiness to exercise moral and religious control has been propagated among priests, pastors, presbyters, and ecclesiastical hierarchs. This has had fateful consequences for the understanding and practice of the Supper, and for church life.

Subjected to moral and religious observation, the Supper could no longer be understood as a feast of reconciliation, a feast of rejoicing in God, and a feast of peace among human beings. Instead it came across to many persons as an anxiety-producing means of moral gatekeeping. In a sad irony, the feast of unconditional acceptance of human beings by God and among each other was misused for intrahuman moral control!

If someone went to communion frequently, they "seemed to need it"! Or the pious self-righteous Christians seemed to be demonstrating their perfect self-examination and "worthiness," inasmuch as they frequently went to communion. By contrast, many "poor souls" tormented themselves in confession and in somber, paralyzing "self-examinations" which did little to provide clear answers: Shall I take part in the meal? May I take part in the meal? Have I rightly "judged myself"? Or am I "drawing judgment" upon myself if I eat "unworthily"? Frequently the mixture of sensitive self-torment and condescending clerical control issued in neurotic or cynical attitudes: The whole thing is liable to be nothing but hocus-pocus[1] anyway!

In order to find a way out of this unhealthy error and confusion, two perspectives must be clearly distinguished:

1. This pseudo-Latin magic formula from the sixteenth century presumably is derived from the Latin version of the "words of institution": *Hoc est corpus meum!*

- In the celebration of the Supper, God unconditionally accepts human beings who, in a threatened world, have fallen under the power of sin! This acceptance includes all, even the enemies of communion with Christ!
- At the same time, the church of Christ, the Christians who compose that church, must take care that this meal is celebrated in accordance with the meal's identity. This is Paul's concern. The celebration of the meal must not be manipulated and perverted so that it contradicts its identity. Therefore human beings must judge whether their celebration of the meal is giving expression to this unconditional acceptance of all participants. Where they are contributing to the perversion and misuse of the Supper — for example, through pride and demonstrative lack of love — they should if need be exclude themselves from the Supper, so that they will be "judged" by Christ — and not by anyone else!

The community, the church of Christ, must attend to the right celebration of the Supper. Each person must judge him- or herself. But no one has the power and the authorization to exclude a particular person or a particular group of persons from participation in the Supper! On the contrary, Paul's reproach to the Corinthians applies precisely to a celebration of the Supper which is misused to exercise moral control and for some persons to dominate others: "When you come together, it is not really to eat the Lord's supper!" (1 Cor 11:20).

The First Recipients of Jesus' Supper: Judas, "Who Betrayed Him"; Peter, "Who Denied Him"; the Disciples, "Who Abandoned Him and Fled"

Jesus does not celebrate the last supper with his disciples because they are the small, faithful apostolic elite, the few irreproachable models of integrity, the glorious Twelve, to whom the administration of Jesus' legacy is entrusted on the basis of their moral and religious blamelessness. The disciples do not stand above the threatened world. Rather, they participate in it. They are no less exposed to it than are the persons with whom they are in the future supposed to celebrate the meal "in remembrance" of Jesus. The disciples are themselves enmeshed in the "night of betrayal."

In the Coptic church there is supposedly the legend that Judas leaves the table fellowship before the meal. Yet there is not one single reference in the biblical texts that would suggest that Judas is excluded from the meal. To be sure, he is identified as "betrayer." To be sure, we read that "it would have been better for that one not to have been born!" (Mk 14:21; Mt 26:24). Yet nothing, absolutely nothing, suggests that Judas is hindered in participating in the communal celebration of the meal. This is likewise the case for Peter, who will betray Jesus three times, for the disciples who will fall asleep in Gethsemane, and for the disciples in general, who will become embroiled in controversies over rank, and who ultimately will all abandon Jesus and flee.

The acceptance of the community's enemies and of sinners, which is characteristic of the pre-Easter Jesus' practice of table fellowship, reaches an exemplary apex in Jesus' celebration of the last supper. Here what happens is not only "mercy" as the acceptance of the marginalized and suffering. Here what happens is "mercy" as gracious regard for human beings who call into question, cancel, and dissolve communion with God and among each other. Here what happens is acceptance "of sinners," for the biblical texts call "sinners" human beings who, consciously or unconsciously, cut themselves and others off from God, thereby bringing themselves and others into situations of need and distress (cf. esp. chapters 6 and 10).

Unconditional Acceptance: The Supper Must Not Be Misused for the Purposes of Moral or Church Disciplinary Control

These insights make clear the dangers which proceed from a moralization of the celebration of the Supper — dangers which, at least in Western traditions, have often enough come to pass. In the celebration of the Supper there is a strict interconnection between: (1) the expressed will for justice (inasmuch as all participants are placed on an equal footing in the celebration of the meal); (2) the acceptance not only of the weak, but also of sinners; and (3) thanksgiving to God the creator for God's goodness, preservation, and deliverance.[2] All celebrations of the Supper that do not ex-

2. Cultic life (the act of giving thanks and glory to God, as well as the search for knowledge of God and for knowledge of God's intentions with creation), justice (in the sense of the announcement of a basic will for justice in the symbolic celebration of the meal, which places all participants on an equal footing), and mercy (in the acceptance of the weak and of sinners) — these are all basic specifications of God's law, and here they work together in an exemplary way. Cf. M. Welker, *God the Spirit,* trans. John F. Hoffmeyer (Minneapolis: Fortress, 1994), *passim.*

press this interconnection, the unity of these intentions, are inappropriate *anaxíōs* (1 Cor 11:27). All practices that obscure this interconnection make human beings "unworthy" (again: *anaxíōs*) to receive.

Once we perceive how holy communion unfolds against the background of the "night of self-giving and betrayal," it becomes impossible to cast doubt upon the fundamental acceptance of sinners in the Supper. It is incompatible with the Supper to have human beings sitting in judgment over each other and deciding which supposedly righteous person is admitted to the Supper and which "unworthy" person is excluded. It is a total perversion of communion to turn it into a process of judgment by some persons over others, or to use it to support such an undertaking. The Supper is not a test case for the moral self-assertion of a community. It is not a religious opportunity to render or refuse moral or judicial recognition to other human beings.

The self-denominated "righteous" who want to sit in judgment over others must instead judge whether *they themselves* are taking seriously the radicality and breadth of the reconciling work of God and Jesus Christ in the Supper! They themselves are celebrating the Supper "unworthily" and "for their own judgment" when they obscure and fail to recognize the following fact: In the Supper which Jesus celebrates with his disciples, the broken bread and the cup of the new covenant are also extended to Judas Iscariot, who hands Jesus over, and to Peter, who betrays him.

We must not separate the celebration of the eucharist (that is, the thanksgiving to God) from the celebration of the communal meal, the grateful celebration of the reconciliation of human beings with God and the symbolic reconciliation of humans with each other. The celebration of the Supper is concerned with building up the body of Christ: specifically, in the form of the celebration of a communal meal in which thanksgiving to the Creator and the breaking and sharing of bread for friends and foes are essentially bound together. The thanksgiving to the Creator and the symbolically explicit will for basic justice are tied to the recognition that this process does not stop short of the community's enemies. Jesus celebrates the Supper with his disciples, to whom he says: "You will all become deserters because of me" (Mt 26:31; Mk 14:27). It is precisely these disciples who are commissioned to repeat this celebration in his memory, and to pass the practice along. But this means: Neither an individual nor a community can pass the judgment to exclude human beings from holy communion on the basis of moral, religious, or other defects, failures, and crimes. Only Christ himself judges, so that the only possible exclusion from the celebration of the Supper is a *self-exclusion* oriented on the will of Christ. But this self-exclusion is appropriate only in extreme cases, in which the manner of one's own participation in the celebration of the meal obscures its meaning. The Corinthians offer an example of this.

In What Does the "Unworthy Eating and Drinking" in Corinth Consist?

First Interpretation: Unsocially Separated in Sharing the Meal — but Nevertheless Bound Together in the Eucharistic Community

In the 11th chapter of the first letter to the Corinthians Paul begins by describing the problem: The Corinthians are celebrating a "Supper" that in truth is not the Supper of Jesus Christ.

1 Corinthians 11:17, 20-22:

17 Now in the following instructions I do not commend you, because when you come together it is not for the better but for the worse.

20 When you come together, it is not really to eat the Lord's supper.

21 For when the time comes to eat, each of you goes ahead with your own supper (alternative translation: each one of you takes out his or her own food), and one goes hungry and another becomes drunk.

22 What! Do you not have homes to eat and drink in? Or do you show contempt for the church of God and humiliate those who have nothing? What should I say to you? Should I commend you? In this matter I do not commend you!

Paul then cites in 1 Corinthians 11:23-26 the tradition he received of the "institution of the Supper":

23 For I received from the Lord what I also handed on to you, that the Lord Jesus on the night when he was betrayed took a loaf of bread,

24 and when he had given thanks, he broke it and said, "This is my body that is for you. Do this in remembrance of me."

25 In the same way he took the cup also, after supper, saying, "This cup is the new covenant in my blood. Do this, as often as you drink it, in remembrance of me."
26 For as often as you eat this bread and drink the cup, you proclaim the Lord's death until he comes.

Measured by this standard, the Corinthians are celebrating a perverted Supper to their own harm, unworthily, for their own judgment. They are making themselves "answerable for the body and blood of the Lord." Paul asserts this in 1 Corinthians 11:27-29, 31-34.

27 Whoever, therefore, eats the bread or drinks the cup of the Lord in an unworthy manner will be answerable for the body and blood of the Lord.
28 Examine youselves, and only then eat of the bread and drink of the cup.
29 For all who eat and drink without discerning the body, eat and drink judgment against themselves. . . .
31 But if we judged ourselves, we would not be judged.
32 But when we are judged by the Lord, we are disciplined so that we may not be condemned along with the world.
33 So then, my brothers and sisters, when you come together to eat, wait for one another (alternative translation: wait on one another!).
34 If you are hungry, eat at home, so that when you come together, it will not be for your judgment. About the other things I will give instructions when I come.

What exactly is the Corinthians' failure? Why and in what way are they celebrating the Supper "unworthily" and "for their judgment"?

New Testament scholarship provides us with two interpretations, which are distinguished from each other only by a subtlety of translation, but which result in two very different pictures. The first interpretation assumes that already in the time of Paul the church in Corinth was first eating a meal to satiate hunger, and then celebrating the Supper. According to this interpretation, the actual meal (later called "agape") had already been separated (see, however, chapter 1 for evidence to the contrary) from the religious rite (later designated as "eucharist"). This consensus of many New Testament scholars conceives the situation in Corinth in something like the following manner:

> At an evening hour . . . people come together in an appropriate room. . . . The members of the community who are better off financially, whose time is more at their own disposal, arrive earlier. They bring provisions with them which are supposed to suffice for all, but they begin to eat and drink for themselves, and soon are in a jolly mood. Slaves and wage laborers are not allowed to leave earlier from the household of their master or from their workplace. When they come somewhat later, they find only bits and pieces left of the full meal, to which they have nothing to contribute from their own means. At the end of the meal is the double sacramental action over bread and wine. The more highly placed Corinthians try to placate their own conscience and others with the argument that no one is excluded from receiving the sacrament, which is ultimately all that matters.[3]

From this perspective, Paul's reproach would be as follows: Some are taking part — to the point of drunkenness — in a full meal in which hunger plays a defining role. They should be so good as to hold this meal at home, prior to engaging in religious communion with those who are poor.

Second Interpretation: Demonstrative Self-Absorption and Social Brutality in Connection with the Misuse of the Supper

In a subtle investigation, New Testament scholar Otfried Hofius has carefully reconstructed the course of the meal celebration that was confronting Paul in Corinth. Hofius begins by criticizing the consensus that says that in Corinth the full meal and the Supper had already been separated. He shows that the social indifference and brutality in Corinth attain greater depths than seen by the first interpretation, precisely because they do not stop short of the Supper. The full meal and the Supper are still bound together in Corinth. Egotistic self-absorption and a tolerated equality of all in the worship service do not stand side by side — with whatever moral duplicity! Instead the unsocial behavior is demonstrated

3. Otfried Hofius, "Herrenmahl und Herrenmahlsparadosis: Erwägungen zu 1 Kor 11,23b-25," in *Paulusstudien,* 2nd ed., WUNT 51 (Tübingen: Mohr, 1994), p. 207, citing H.-J. Klauck, *1 Corinthians,* Neue Echter Bibel 7, 2nd ed. (Würzburg, 1987), p. 81.

in the midst of the celebration of the Supper, which in Paul's time included the full meal.

Two points are decisive for this interpretation: What form did the Supper have in Corinth, and how are verses 21 and 23 of 1 Corinthians 11 translated?

Hofius first notes that Jesus' actions in the last supper, which for Paul forms the background here (1 Cor 11:23ff.), "show the typical ritual elements of a Jewish meal. The words: He took the bread, spoke the prayer of thanks, and broke it, describe in characteristically Jewish terminology the rite of the table prayer before the meal. . . . With the breaking of the bread, which the person giving the blessing then distributes to the table companions, the meal is begun. The conclusion of the meal consists in . . . the prayer of thanksgiving at table after the meal. That is precisely what verse 25 is talking about." Nor does the reference to the "cup after supper" by any means argue against a "normal" Jewish meal. "The 'cup of blessing,' which the rabbinic literature can also characterize simply as 'the cup' when the context is clear, is always . . . the cup with wine, over which the table prayer is spoken after the meal." By no means is the cup of blessing used only at the Passover meal, or only at Jewish festival meals. In accordance with Jewish table customs, it belongs at every meal in which wine is drunk. Hofius gives a whole list of passages that refer to the cup — "over which words of praise are spoken" — after the meal, and which relate to the — undeniably festive — conclusion of a daily meal.[4]

In 1 Corinthians 11 — the oldest of the texts concerning the Supper that have been passed down to us — nothing argues for the particularities of a Passover meal, while everything argues for a normal Jewish meal (see especially chapter 3). After intensive critical engagement with differing interpretations, Hofius concludes that the "ritual actions depicted here correspond, rather, to the form of the table prayers before and after the meal, such as are typical of a Jewish meal."[5] On the basis of the consideration of further linguistic details, Hofius insists that the tradition presupposed by Paul could only be a meal between an action with the bread and an action with the cup. "Historically speaking, there cannot be the least doubt concerning the existence of a celebration of the Lord's supper, in

4. Hofius, "Herrenmahl," p. 212.

5. Hofius, "Herrenmahl," p. 214. Hofius regards it as impossible that the words "after the supper" could also be applied to the breaking of the bread, since the breaking of bread is a fixed ritual for beginning a meal.

which a full meal had its place between the ritual with the bread and the ritual with the cup."[6]

What, then, is the perversion of the Supper which makes its celebration "unworthy" and "for judgment"? Is it somehow not enough to reproach the Corinthians for selfishly satisfying their own hunger and for drinking beyond the requirements of thirst before the Supper is celebrated with the later-arriving poor? Is the problem somehow not adequately addressed with Paul's reproach (1 Cor 11:21) that each person is going ahead with his or her own meal, and that one person is going hungry while the next person is already drunk before the religious celebration gets underway?

Hofius shows that the decisive Greek word in 1 Corinthians 11:21 need not be understood temporally as "taking ahead of time," but can also be used to mean "taking out"! Then the reproach would clearly be that each person is taking out his or her own food at the meal and consuming it. Each person is consuming what he or she brought! Only on this basis does it become possible to understand the statements that each person should act in such a way that a communal meal could take place.

Inasmuch as the rich consume the means of nourishment that they themselves have brought, the social tensions are clearly emphasized. "In light of the callously oblivious behavior of the rich, the poor 'are once again reminded of their oppressive situation.'"[7] This is what constitutes the "unworthiness" of the way in which the meal is celebrated! Instead of demonstrating mutual acceptance and justice in the celebration of the Supper, the perverted meal becomes a sign and demonstration of inequality and injustice!

There remains an important objection to this view. Doesn't verse 33 say: "When you come together to eat, wait for one another"? Hofius shows, though, that while the Greek expression can indeed mean "wait for someone," it can also mean "welcome someone, show hospitality to someone, wait on someone." And precisely this expression: "Wait hospitably on one another, serve one another," belongs in a table fellowship. Hofius comments that the expression "wait on one another" "would be fundamentally misunderstood if one wanted to interpret it to mean: The hungry rich should satisfy their hunger at home before the beginning of

6. Hofius, "Herrenmahl," p. 216.

7. Hofius, "Herrenmahl," p. 220, with a quotation from Chr. Wolff, *Der erste Brief des Paulus an die Korinther,* vol. 2: *Auslegung der Kapitel 8–16,* Theologisches Handkommentar VII/2 (Berlin, 1982), p. 81.

the worship service, so that at the gathering for worship itself they can wait until the poor members of the community have also arrived."[8]

Paul's instructions are thus clearly aimed at the distinction between a private meal and holy communion. Anyone who is primarily concerned with eating should eat at home. However, Paul is not entering a plea for the (subsequent) separation of the full meal and the sacrament. His discussion applies to a ritual meal celebrated by the community, in which the rite with the bread, the full meal, and the rite with the cup still belong together. "This celebration is constituted as 'Lord's supper' by the 'Lord's bread' . . . and the 'Lord's cup' . . . that is, by the two sacramental acts which bracket the communal meal, at the same time qualifying it in its very essence."[9] This celebration of the meal must not be perverted into a demonstration of injustice and unmercifulness. Here human beings must "wait on one another," lovingly and justly sharing the means of nourishment that have been brought. Otherwise the celebration happens "for their judgment."

Precisely the interconnection between the full meal and the Supper can call attention to distortions and perversions that are no longer so clear in celebrations of the meal which are more strongly symbolic. The question "Do you want to humiliate those who do not have anything?" calls attention to the "unworthiness" of the celebration of the meal. It calls attention to the fact that the meal and those who are celebrating it are "unworthy" as soon as intrahuman disrespect perverts the act of giving thanks and glory to God. The celebration of the meal happens "for judgment" when egotistic, indifferent, and brutal forms of behavior not only injure fellow human beings, but at the same time pervert and make a laughingstock of Christ's intentions in instituting the meal. Under such conditions the community comes together "for the worse" and "for judgment."

How Is the Supper Celebrated "Worthily"? The Tension Between "Acceptance of the Weak" and the Preservation of Cultic Form: When Apparently Secondary Things Like Grape Juice, Individual Glasses, and Wafers Become Warning Signals

Against the background described above, it becomes clear that the form in which the Supper is celebrated is by no means a peripheral issue. Precisely in

8. Hofius, "Herrenmahl," p. 221.

9. Hofius, "Herrenmahl," p. 223.

a so concentratedly symbolic action, every detail can in principle become a cause for "offense." Whether supposedly or in fact, little gestures can express deficient mutual acceptance, can demonstrate inequality or injustice, or can wound the sensibilities of the weak, and thereby pervert the Supper. Therefore cultic clarity and integrity are important. Therefore experiments with "new forms" should take place only with extreme caution, and not without an extensive process of congregational consultation in which members of the church community have the opportunity to respond to the proposed changes (see especially chapters 9 and 10). Here, if not before, one can understand why many churches place such great value on overall pastoral oversight and supervision precisely with regard to the Supper. One can see looming on the horizon here a basic conflict that simply cannot be avoided in a living congregation and church: tension can and does arise over and over again between, on the one hand, the preservation of the clear form of the sacramental celebration and, on the other hand, the equal participation of all, especially the acceptance of minorities. This brings us to the so-called grape juice question.

At first glance the question "May we or should we celebrate holy communion with (red) grape juice as well?" can appear laughable. Grape juice, too, does not come into being without the interaction of nature and culture: it is a "gift of creation." It is also a festive drink. And it can symbolize Christ's blood. Where is the problem, then? In addition, if we consider that, by using wine, we make it difficult or impossible for persons suffering from alcoholism to participate in the Supper, the use of grape juice would appear to be practically a "command of the Lord." Do you want to humiliate those who have alcohol problems? However, things are not quite that simple.

If we lived in a culture which had grape juice as a festive drink, but not wine, we could simply replace wine with grape juice, since the alcohol content is obviously not the point of the celebration of the meal. We would then have correctly "translated" what the biblical texts intend. But in replacing wine with grape juice we intervene in a way that, for the cultic consciousness of some persons, introduces a distortion: a specific problem of acceptance and welcome — namely, the acceptance of persons suffering from alcoholism — is pushed to the center, at least for some of the participants in the Supper. This pushes to the sidelines the problem of the acceptance and welcome of those who insist on celebrating the Supper as "literally" as possible in accordance with Scripture, and who are not strong enough to accept alternatives for the benefit of the weak.

Behind this problem — that we have various "weaknesses" in the community which all in principle need acceptance and compensation — lies another problem. This problem becomes clear if we include in our reflections the problem "common cup or individual glasses," and other problems of the "correct celebration of the meal."

Due to fear of contagious diseases or to anxieties about imaginary dangers, many congregations no longer use the common cup, or no longer use only the common cup. In many congregations individual glasses are the only option, while numerous others offer individual glasses as the "first choice," so that the common cup is offered only "as desired": that is, only if a participant explicitly indicates that preference. Even many who are "faithful to Scripture," and who insist on "wine" as an element, prefer a little glass for individual use. In the process an important sign of commonality is lost. Yet we must not ignore the anxieties about contagious diseases. These weaknesses must also be accepted with love. Nor can we simply pass over with a condescending smile the weaknesses of those for whom crumbly bread is a problem and who therefore prefer wafers, and the weaknesses of those for whom the wafers are as repulsive as individual glasses and who want to really break bread. At first glance these issues seem only to repeat the grape juice problem. But the multiplicity of possible difficulties signals that more is at stake: namely, consideration for the various anxieties, scruples, and weaknesses can result in the disintegration of the Supper's form in two different directions.

Ritualistic correctness can result in a brutal and unworthy celebration of the Supper. "Anyone with alcohol problems or hysterical fears about contagious diseases should just not come!" Such an ideology of the hard and undaunted destroys the Supper.

But an inflation of sensitive measures of special consideration can also pervert the meal to the point of unworthy celebration. Besides the grape juice issue and the question of individual glasses, one can imagine many problems that could require continual changes in the form in which the Supper is celebrated — from problems with the symbolism of blood to the problem of having trouble enduring the appearance of particular fellow humans. A complete liberation from fears of contagion and from problems of communication would ultimately result in self-service with shrink-wrapped bread and wine while seated in front of a screen showing a video of a holy communion service! This, however, would no longer be a celebration of Christ's Supper.

In these situations of conflict pastoral sensitivity and creativity is necessary — not only on the part of theologians, church councils, and bearers of ministerial office, but on the part of the whole community. We must develop ways of celebrating communion which take account of people's scruples, without destroying the biblically given forms. Nor may a community strive for an optimal form only for the familiar group anticipated at worship. Other Christians who come from outside must also be able to recognize here the Supper in accordance with Christ's words of institution (see especially chapter 9).

The developments with regard to the questions of grape juice and individual glasses demonstrate that these problems are by no means unsolvable. In the "grape juice question" congregations have found solutions by regularly or occasionally announcing and celebrating a "non-alcoholic" Supper, or by offering two cups, one with wine and one with grape juice. Since larger congregations use several cups anyway, there the use of separate cups for wine and grape juice has no discriminatory effect. Family worship services celebrated with grape juice (see chapter 9 on the question of the admission of children to the Supper) also offer tactful forms that make it possible even in small congregations for persons suffering from alcoholism to participate in the Supper without discrimination. With regard to the common cup, the problem could be solved by offering two cups: members of the community who wish to do so can drink communally from one of the cups; those who have concerns of hygiene can dip their bread in the other cup *(intinctio)*. The commonality with regard to the "cup of the new covenant" would still find relatively good expression.

It is advisable neither to downplay and suppress these and other newly emerging problems of the communal celebration of the meal, nor routinely to change the meal practice in the face of every new problem. Without putting each other down and burdening each other, we should repeatedly address, both in preaching and in community conversation, the problems that cause difficulties for us today in the communal celebration of the meal. It is not only alcohol problems and anxieties about contact and contagion which distance us from the communal celebration of the meal. Concerns that our traditions and our solid religious footing could be abandoned in a church adrift in liturgical experimentation can have the same effect. We can accept these anxieties and each other if we recognize that many of these concerns grow out of the honest effort to celebrate the Supper "worthily" with each other, and not "for judgment" and "for the worse."

Results

The acceptance of all persons, which is characteristic of the meals celebrated by the pre-Easter Jesus, reaches an exemplary apex in the Supper. The Supper is a celebration of God's unconditional acceptance of human beings, who in a threatened world have fallen under the power of sin! This acceptance includes all, even the enemies of communion with Christ! (Cf. chapter 2.)

At the same time, the Christians who constitute Christ's church must see to it that holy communion is celebrated in accordance with its specified identity. The celebration of the Supper must not be manipulated or perverted. Therefore persons must "judge" themselves and, if need be, exclude themselves, so that they do not contribute to the perversion of the Supper and so that they will not be "judged" by Christ — and not by anybody else!

Holy communion is not a test case for the moral self-assertion of a community. It is not a religious opportunity to render or refuse moral or judicial recognition to other human beings. Rather, Paul's reproach to the Corinthians applies precisely to a celebration of the Supper which is misused to exercise religious and moral control and for some persons to dominate others: "When you come together, it is not really to eat the Lord's supper!" (1 Cor 11:20).

The Corinthians celebrate the Supper (admittedly in connection with a full meal) "unworthily" and "for their own judgment," inasmuch as some of them act in a self-absorbed, indifferent, and brutal way toward those who are socially weaker. In celebrations of the Supper without a full meal the forms of callousness are more subtle and harder to recognize and remove.

As a contemporary — but not merely "trendy" — example of this problem, we can turn to the tensions between, on the one hand, those who devote their efforts to the acceptance of persons plagued with alcohol problems (grape juice), anxieties about hygiene (individual glasses), and other issues and, on the other hand, those who are worried about transgressing and dissolving biblical, early Christian, and ecumenical forms. In order to confine self-exclusion from the Supper to unusual, extreme cases, we must recognize such tensions between, on the one hand, efforts for loving, mutual acceptance and, on the other hand, efforts to preserve cultic forms in their integrity. The careful, loving, and creative labor on these tensions in the process of shaping the celebration of the Supper is the task of pastors, synods, presbyteries, and above all of congregations as a whole.

PART 2

Holy Communion — Celebration of the Presence of Jesus Christ

CHAPTER 5

"This Is My Body . . . This Is My Blood"

The Much-Disputed "Real Presence" of Christ in the Supper

What happens in holy communion? The fifth answer is: *In holy communion the risen and exalted Christ is present! With him the reconciliation of human beings with God is present, and the reconciliation of humans among themselves becomes effective.* The following chapters strive to make this answer comprehensible and to demonstrate that it is not a bald theological assertion. The second part of this book has as its theme the "bodily" presence of Jesus Christ in holy communion. The purpose of this chapter is to make accessible the difficult notion of the "real presence" of Christ. What have we learned so far that could contribute to clarification?

What Have We Learned up to This Point about the "Real Presence" of Christ? — The Risen One Is Recognized in Thanksgiving and in the Breaking of Bread

(Cf. the section of the Introduction: "The Offensive Reality of the Risen Jesus Christ as the Key to Understanding the Supper.")

According to Luke 24:30-35, the risen Christ is recognized in the thanksgiving over the bread and in the breaking of the bread:

> 30 When he was at the table with them, he took bread, blessed and broke it, and gave it to them.

31 Then their eyes were opened, and they recognized him; and he vanished from their sight.
32 They said to each other, "Were not our hearts burning within us while he was talking to us on the road, while he was opening the scriptures to us?"
33 That same hour they got up and returned to Jerusalem; and they found the eleven and their companions gathered together.
34 They were saying, "The Lord has risen indeed, and he has appeared to Simon!"
35 Then they told what had happened on the road, and how he had been made known to them in the breaking of the bread.

Yet it is not just in the action of breaking bread that the risen Christ can be recognized. On the contrary, a multiplicity of experiences issue in the knowledge that Christ is risen! What is consistent throughout these experiences? What do they have in common with the key experience of opening the meal with praise and the breaking of bread?

The Unity of Reconciliation with God and Reconciliation among Human Beings (Cf. Chapters 1 and 3)

As we saw in the first part of this book, two relationships are renewed in the celebration of holy communion. The relationship of human beings to God is renewed in the giving of thanks and glory, and the relationship of humans to each other is renewed in the symbolic meal community. In whatever fleeting and fragile way: Here is a realization of the announcement of "glory to God in the highest, and peace on earth among humans on whom God's favor rests!"

The meal community expresses not only the will for mutual acceptance and for basic justice. As the community of the Supper it goes out of its way to include even those who threaten and jeopardize it (cf. chapters 2 and 4). In the Supper reconciliation with God and unconditional reconciliation among humans are indissolubly bound together. The reconciliation of human beings with God and reconciliation with each other — even to the point of love for enemies — are essential to the being of Jesus Christ. This double reconciliation summarizes that which is consistently present throughout the most diverse images of Christ and the most various ways of calling Christ to mind.

But does this permit us to speak of Christ's "bodily" and "real" presence?

"Body and Blood": Most Concrete, Perceivable Vitality and Most Internal Vital Power

How are we to understand the statements: "This is my body; this is my blood"? This difficult question has repeatedly been answered to the effect that here "the whole Christ" is present. But without further clarification, this answer remains a riddle.

According to biblical understanding, the power of life is in the blood. If the blood is "poured out," the body returns "to dust." The body is the bearer, the container of this vital power found in the blood. Without body and blood we — on earth, as earthly beings — cannot live. But body and blood are not only bound to us in the most intimate way as guarantors and bearers of our earthly life. They also make it possible for us to be seen and known from the outside, as healthy or injured persons. "Body and blood" is certainly not all that can be perceived about us and that can be said of us. But body and blood constitute our externally perceivable, earthly vitality, and our most concrete, internal vital power. In the Supper, Jesus identifies his externally perceivable, earthly vitality and his most concrete, internal vital power with the bread and the wine: I am giving you that in which I live here on earth!

"Body and Blood" and the Freely Given Gifts of Creation of Bread and Wine (Cf. Chapter 3)

Yet how do the body and blood of Jesus Christ, which are "given up" in his crucifixion, hang together with the bread and the wine that we give and take in celebrating the Supper? How do the body and blood of Christ hang together with the bread and wine in the Supper, which we can perceive with our senses — thus in a completely bodily and real way — and which we can even take into ourselves? The history of the attempts to give a definitive answer to this question concerning the "elements" of bread and wine is long and full of conflict. The words that Jesus speaks, the words that the priest speaks, the words that the gathered community speaks — these words must do something to the elements which leads to the real presence of Christ.

In contrast to this approach, burdened with problems and conflicts, we have begun by attempting to understand the internal constitution of bread and wine as gifts of creation which must be regarded as gifts brimming with blessing. Proceeding from the successful interaction of the powers of nature and of human culture, these gifts of bread and wine are unthinkable without God's creative goodness and without the activity of God's Spirit. The fact that bread and wine are present — however unprepossessing this might be — points to these divine powers. Thanks is given to God for these gifts of creation, and in the communal meal human beings give each other a share in these gifts. Yet this still does not measure the full dimensions of Christ's Supper. We must understand his presence as the giver of the gifts of creation, and as the actual gift!

To this end the twentieth-century ecumenical conversations — more precisely, the intra-Protestant conversations — have taken an important step forward. A bold "leap" in the theology of the Supper has liberated us from being mesmerized by "the elements," even to the point of concentrating exclusively on them. Admittedly, this bold leap did not yet provide a completely satisfying answer to the question concerning the real presence of Christ in the Supper. But it did open up a new approach. It opened up this new approach by means of the idea of "personal presence."

The "Personal Presence" of Christ: How the Lutheran-Reformed Discussion of the Supper Found Its Way out of a Dead-End Street

- The bread *is* the body of Christ *(est).*
- The bread *signifies* the body of Christ *(significat).*

In 1529 in Marburg, the attempt to achieve unity between the Reformers Luther *(est)* and Zwingli *(significat)* shipwrecked on this difference.[1] Only in the twentieth century have Lutherans and Reformed overcome the fixed division between them. This was possible because it became clear that we must not allow ourselves to be transfixed by the so-called elements. Instead we must take the following as our starting points:

1. Cf. T. Kaufmann, "Abendmahl II. Kirchengeschichtlich, 3. Reformation," in *Die Religion in Geschichte und Gegenwart,* vol. 1, 4th ed. (Tübingen: Mohr, 1998), pp. 24ff.

1. When Christ identifies bread and wine with his body and blood, he identifies both of them with himself.
2. It is only in the overall context of the celebration of the meal that the elements of bread and wine are what they are.

We cannot adequately appreciate bread and wine as communion "elements" apart from their function and their significance in the shared symbolic meal of the gathered community. In the first part of this book we have tried to take to heart this advance in understanding. Now we must enter into the logic of what it means to say that bread and wine are not "elements" of the Supper apart from their unity with Christ "in person."

The external occasion of clarifying the doctrinal differences between members of the Lutheran, Reformed, and Union churches in Germany was their common resistance in the Confessing Church. The Christians bound together in resistance against National Socialism suffered under their separation in the understanding and celebration of the Supper. The Second Meeting of the Fourth Confessing Synod of the Evangelical Church of the Old Prussian Union in Halle in 1937 attempted "to find a basis for a theologically grounded communion fellowship."[2] The model was the Barmen Theological Declaration with its strict concentration on Jesus Christ, "the one Word of God." The fact that Calvin's doctrine of the Supper offered a mediating position was also helpful in unifying the churches of the Reformation.

The central biblical text, the basis of union which the Synod takes as its starting point, is 1 Corinthians 10:16-17:

> 16 The cup of blessing that we bless, is it not a sharing in the blood of Christ? The bread that we break, is it not a sharing in the body of Christ?
> 17 Because there is one bread, we who are many are one body, for we all partake of the one bread.

The corresponding wording of the declaration is as follows:

> In view of the pressing question whether, in the eyes of scripture and of the confessions that witness to scripture, we Lutheran, Reformed,

2. Lessing, *Abendmahl,* Bensheimer Ökumenische Studienhefte 1 (Göttingen: Vandenhoeck, 1993), p. 20. The text of the Synod is in Niemöller, *Synode zu Halle 1937.*

and Union Christians act rightly if we celebrate holy communion with each other, the Synod places itself under the word of holy scripture from 1 Corinthians 10:16-17:

> The blessed cup that we bless, is it not communion in the blood of Christ? The bread that we break, is it not communion in the body of Christ? For it is one bread, so that we who are many are one body, since we all partake of the one bread.[3]

Eckhard Lessing has summarized the decisive accomplishments of the Old Prussian Confessing Synod of Halle in 1937:

1. "The concept of the *personal presence* (of Christ) takes the place of the concepts of real presence or spiritual presence. The unity of Christ's person and work is emphasized."[4]
2. On this basis, the Synod insists that Jesus Christ is the *giver* in the Supper. Jesus Christ is also the *gift* in the Supper.
3. The Synod emphasizes that the Supper is a communal meal, a meal that grounds community. "In contrast to an individualistic understanding of holy communion that had wide currency at the time, here attention is drawn to the ecclesiological relevance of the Supper. In doing so the Halle theses implicitly open themselves to the ecumenical church. Moreover, they do so in a way that points to the unity and communion of the churches as something that already exists, rather than as something that must still be brought into existence. The Supper constitutes the church, and not vice versa."[5]

These decisions represent the acquisition of a new basis for understanding. The Synod concludes that it testifies "with one mind: . . . Jesus Christ, our Lord and Savior, who came in the flesh for our sake, who once offered himself on the cross for us, and who rose bodily from

3. This first push forward was picked up by the discussion concerning the Supper between the German Evangelical churches in the years 1947-57, which culminated with the so-called Arnoldshain Theses on the Supper. With regard to analogous conversations in some other parts of the ecumenical church, see M. Lienhard, *Lutherisch-reformierte Kirchengemeinschaft heute: Der Leuenberger Konkordienentwurf im Kontext der bisherigen lutherisch-reformierten Dialoge,* 2nd ed. (Frankfurt: Lembeck, 1973), pp. 9ff., 16ff., 25ff.

4. Lessing, *Abendmahl,* p. 24; emphasis added.

5. Lessing, *Abendmahl,* p. 24.

death, is himself the gift of grace of his community's Supper, instituted by him."[6]

The Synod cleverly distinguishes between two things:

1. The *shared certainty of faith:* Jesus Christ is present in person in the Supper, and communicates himself!
2. The *still regnant differences of doctrine* concerning the "manner of the Lord's self-communication in the Supper." The Synod emphasizes, however, that the differences are not about the fact "that the Lord himself is the gift of the Supper." The gift is the giver; the giver is the gift.

On account of the persistent differences concerning the manner of Christ's self-communication in the Supper, the Second Church Assembly in Treysa in 1947 decided to carry out a binding theological conversation between the Protestant churches concerning the doctrine of holy communion. This conversation was marked by the consistent return to New Testament texts. This *biblical orientation* has retained a defining role in the Protestant contributions concerning the Supper in the wider ecumenical debate.

It is practically impossible to imagine the ecumenical discussions of the twentieth century without the steps forward taken by the Synod of Halle in 1937. Nevertheless, the idea articulated there of Christ's "personal presence" remains unclear. As we see today, it represents only an intermediate stage that is not yet able to take over from the Reformation notion of the "real presence."

Toward a Deepening of the Notion of "Personal Presence"

When we say that a human being is "personally present," as a rule we mean that this person is with us "as a whole," in her full identity. Not merely an image, a letter, a representative, a shared conception or memory, but this human being is *bodily* present. Naturally we are at least subconsciously aware that even in the actual living and concrete presence of a person, even when we think we know her "through and through," we only have aspects, parts, or perspectives of this person present. Yet when

6. Niemöller, *Synode zu Halle 1937,* p. 441.

we say that this person is personally present, we assume that, with these experiences and insights, we can "exhaust" this person. She is present with all her possibilities.

Christian piety is shaped by a wealth of personal relations to the pre-Easter, crucified, and risen Christ. Traditions, confessions, and dogmatics limit and focus the wealth of possible perspectives on Christ, the wealth of his aspects, in order to allow "the person of Christ" really to emerge in these relations as clearly and completely as possible. Nevertheless, even where we take our orientation from the preformed remembrances, there are very different understandings and images of Christ.

In his book *Jesus Through the Centuries: His Place in the History of Culture,*[7] Jaroslav Pelikan has collected many such historically important images and conceptions of Christ. In specific situations and circles, they claimed to grasp "the whole person," "the whole Christ." These images and conceptions form a very rich mosaic: Jesus the rabbi, Jesus the turning point of history, Jesus the light of the nations, Jesus the king of kings, the cosmic Christ, the Human One, the true image of God, the crucified Christ, the monastic Jesus who rules the world, the bridegroom of the soul, the image of the true human being, the true expression of God, the mirror of eternity, the prince of peace, the teacher of healthy common sense, the one who gives expression to the spirit, the liberator, the one who leads into discipleship, etc. We could easily highlight other typical images and aspects that could be regarded as the "whole Jesus Christ" — at least at specific times and in specific regions of the world. What does this have to do with the personal presence of Jesus in holy communion?

Jesus identifies his body with the bread over which thanksgiving is said to God, and which is then divided and given away. In doing so, Jesus concentrates the many possible aspects of and perspectives on his person on a complex, essential, interconnected process. Jesus puts himself inside the skin of his disciples. He foresees not only their evil deeds. He also sees their helplessness and their lostness. He wants to lead them out of this situation. Through the evil, the betrayal, the slander, the helplessness, and the despair, he wills to be with them, among them, indeed *in* them. In every respect, he wills to strengthen them, to comfort them, to help them up, and to help them through. "In the night of betrayal, slander, and flight, and in the knowledge (or premonition) that the disciples would

7. J. Pelikan, *Jesus Through the Centuries: His Place in the History of Culture* (New Haven: Yale University Press, 1985).

not come through, Jesus gives them this sign of forgiveness as equipment for their journey. When they have fallen, they are to remember and hold fast to this sign."[8]

However, bread and wine are given to the disciples not only for their own support and for their own strengthening. The disciples are also supposed to distribute them and share them with others "in remembrance of Christ" (see especially chapter 8). By means of the identification with bread and wine, the crucified and risen Christ thus becomes present beyond the circle of the disciples. What finds expression in this identification with bread and wine is the creative gift of self for the good of others, the free, creative act of putting oneself inside the skin of others. In the bread distributed during the meal celebrated in remembrance of Christ's self-giving, that which is essential and decisive about Christ's person, the truth of Christ's person, is made present in a concentrated way.

This does not mean that the wealth of perspectives on Christ's person named above are thereby excluded. But they are gathered, concentrated, and bound together in this bread and in this wine, so that in the strictest sense of the word it is correct to say: This bread and this wine hold present in a sensuous, earthly, and bodily way the fullness of the person and presence of Christ, which we otherwise have "in the word."[9]

Back to "Real Presence": The Essential Being of Jesus Christ and the Fullness of His Person in a Certainty Given to the Senses

In holy communion it is not simply the earthly, pre-Easter Jesus of Nazareth who is present in some "revivified" way. To be sure, he and his activ-

8. W. Härle, *Dogmatik* (Berlin: De Gruyter, 1995), p. 562.

9. This has been very clearly emphasized by the conversations between, on the one hand, Anglicans and Methodists, and on the other hand, Anglicans and Roman Catholics, as these conversations have been defined by the interest in "not playing off against one another" the presence in word and the presence in sacrament. "Christ in the fullness of His being, human and divine, crucified and risen, is present in this sacrament" ("Denver Report" 1971 [M-RC], p. 326; cf. "Windsor Statement" 1971 [A-RC], *pp. 7, 70, and "Dublin Report" 1971 [M-RC], pp. 352-53). In this sense the formulation "real presence means personal presence" is persuasive, although from another perspective it could lead to misunderstanding (Gottfried W. Locher, *Streit unter Gästen: Die Lehre aus der Abendmahlsdebatte der Reformatoren für das Verständnis und die Feier des Abendmahles heute,* Theologische Studien 110 [Zurich: TVZ, 1972], p. 16).

ity, suffering, and dying are intensively remembered. To be sure, the Supper attends to the continuity of his earthly life with the life of the risen Christ. But the one who is bodily present in the Supper is the risen Christ. The risen Christ encompasses the entire life of the pre-Easter Jesus; the pre-Easter Jesus is effectively present in the risen Christ. It is the risen Christ who now is with all those to whom he promised his presence "always, to the end of the age" (Mt 28:20).[10] Christ is not present in the Supper "in the same manner that he was present in his earthly life. . . . [His presence does not simply follow] the physical laws of this world. What is here affirmed is a sacramental presence in which God uses realities of this world to convey the realities of the new creation: bread for this life becomes the bread of eternal life."[11] But how can this risen Christ, who encompasses the entire fullness of the person of Jesus Christ, who encompasses everything which he is for "his own" — how can this risen Christ be bodily and really present? It is to this question that the identification of bread and wine with Christ's body and blood replies!

By means of the identification: "This is my body; This is my blood," Christ in the Supper places his externally perceptible, corporeal vitality and his most concrete, inner power of life into the "elements" of the Supper. It is not with bread and wine in themselves that he gives that through which he henceforth lives, as the Risen One, here on earth. Nor do a piece of bread and a cup of wine over which the words of institution are spoken provide in themselves that wherein the risen Christ is really present in what is essential about his person.

It is, rather, the celebration of the interconnection between reconciliation of human beings with God and reconciliation of human beings with each other, carried out as directed by Jesus, which makes bread and wine elements of the presence of the risen Christ, and elements of holy communion. The reality of this twofold process of reconciliation in fact summarizes the decisive being of Jesus Christ. In this process, which — focused on the self-giving of Jesus Christ — in equal measure both praises God and engages in communal giving and taking, eating and drinking, Christ is bodily present. In this celebrated reconciliation with God and in

10. To an increasing degree the ecumenical consensus texts — especially those in which the Orthodox churches collaborate — emphasize that this is inconceivable apart from the presence of God's Spirit. Cf. chapter 12, as well as *God's Reign and Our Unity* 1984 [A-R], p. 43.

11. "Eucharistic Doctrine: Elucidation" 1979 [A-RC], p. 75.

the reconciliation of human beings with each other, Christ is present in a way that is strikingly accessible to sense experience. This communal meal encompasses mutual acceptance, the establishment of basic community, and a demonstration of the will for communal life and for concrete justice. It is in this communal meal, focused on Christ's act of self-giving, that God becomes accessible to sense experience.

However, the real presence of Christ is not exhausted by the essential being of Christ which we experience as strikingly present to the senses. In the celebration of holy communion the "whole Christ" is present — as the pre-Easter Jesus whom we remember, the Crucified One whom we proclaim, the Risen One to whom we bear witness, and the Human One whom we expect and await! This rich and differentiated presence of Christ makes clear that "real presence" is not about a mere object of sense experience, and still less about a christological principle. In the sacramental event of the celebration of the Supper, the gathered community is permeated and surrounded by Christ, by the entire richness of his life. The "real presence" of Christ surrounds the community and the entire church as Christ is made present, remembered, experienced, and awaited in ways that are readily accessible to the senses.

This makes it definitively clear that the so-called elements and the performance of the rite are not self-sufficient. As "elements" and as a cultic performance they depend upon the gathered community, the word of proclamation, the explicit remembrance of Christ, and the clarification of this process.[12] This fact is not a deficiency, but rather an important indication of the particular constitution of Christ's presence. On the one hand, the risen Christ is "not without his own" (Luther). On the other hand, the "real presence" of Christ — like the post-Easter presence of the Risen One (see the Introduction and chapter 9) — is not confined to the concretely gathered community. The gathered community remembers the present and exalted Christ, and awaits his "coming in glory" (his *parousia;* see chapter 7). At the same time, the gathered community acts "in remembrance" of this same Christ in and through the celebration of the meal. In these ways the community relates to a reality of Christ that indeed *fills* the gathered community with its presence, but simultaneously transcends that community.

The notion of Christ's "ubiquity" has been used in an attempt to artic-

12. The fullness of Christ's personal presence finds its correlate in a multitude of experiential perspectives. Cf., e.g., *Towards a Common Understanding* 1990 [R-RC], pp. 223-24, as well as the subsequent chapters of part 2 of this book.

ulate this state of affairs. However, the word is easily misunderstood. Somewhat crude types could rightly embarrass theology and piety with retorts about whether Christ was then "present" in every pants button and in every piece of gravel. In the effort to understand "real presence," we must not attach ourselves to vague conceptions of "the whole" and of "everything." Instead we must focus on word and sacrament in general, and on the Supper in particular: on its breadth, on its radiating influence and the connected presence of Christ "in all the world."[13] Instead of a miraculous "ubiquity," what we encounter is the universality of the "real presence" of Christ as his being and activity overflow with blessing: "All 'grace and truth' (Jn 1:14) are now in our midst."[14]

In this context it is important to recognize that the reality of Christ is not confined to the concretely gathered community. Here (as in the resurrection texts) we must simultaneously focus on the presence of Christ experienced only with the senses and the heavenly reality of the risen and exalted Christ. The texts that are important for the celebration of holy communion repeatedly insist on this simultaneity of sensuous proximity and of the exalted Christ's transcendence of our control. Christ comes into the utmost proximity to persons celebrating the Supper, without thereby denying or obscuring Christ's distance, his being beyond our reach, his death, and his still future coming (see chapters 6 and 7). In the real presence in the Supper, Christ's distance includes and transcends proximity, and Christ's proximity includes and transcends distance. It is the task and the opportunity of the theology and piety of the Supper to perceive this peculiar distance and proximity of Christ. For this purpose the category of "personal presence" is inadequate. It does not do a good job of articulating the breadth and distance of Christ's presence. Nor does it do a good job of articulating his proximity to our senses in bread and wine.

13. Cf. "The Presence of Christ" 1977 [R-RC], pp. 452-54, as well as the well-placed insistence that this presence must be understood in the framework of trinitarian theology (see esp. chapter 12). Picking up on the Reformers, Brian Gerrish helpfully discusses the relations between the presence of the exalted Christ "in heaven," the presence of Christ in the communion elements, and the "ecclesial presence" of Christ (*Grace and Gratitude: The Eucharistic Theology of John Calvin* [Minneapolis: Fortress, 1993], pp. 182ff.). The question of the extent to which the notion of "mystical presence" (157ff.) is valid christologically and in terms of the theology of the Supper must be postponed until another occasion.

14. "The Eucharist" 1978 [L-RC], p. 194, connected with the note that "the eucharistic celebration reflects the phases of salvation history."

In the following chapters, we shall concretize from manifold perspectives the perception of the proximity and distance of Christ present in the Supper. This differentiated perception is indispensable if we do not wish to ignore the depths of human distance from God — depths which Christ promises to bridge and to plumb with his presence. This perception is also indispensable if we wish to know the worth and high standing that are granted to human beings through communion with Christ and through participation in his powers of life. Holy communion celebrates the victorious overcoming, rich in blessings, of human resistance to God's presence. It also celebrates the attendant festive, peaceful communion of human beings with one another. And the celebration turns on Christ's self-giving for human beings becoming present to the senses by means of bread and wine.

Results

In light of the threat from National Socialism, German Union, Lutheran, and Reformed Christians took a bold step in Halle in 1937 in order to lay to rest the Reformation conflicts about Christ's presence in the Supper, and to make it possible to celebrate the Supper together. They distinguished between:

1. The shared certainty of faith: Jesus Christ is present in person in the Supper, and communicates himself! Christ is giver and gift.
2. The still regnant differences of doctrine concerning the "manner of the Lord's self-communication in the Supper," which are not about the fact "that the Lord himself is the gift of the Supper."

On the basis of this shared certainty concerning the "personal presence," first German and European Protestantism (Arnoldshain and Leuenberg), then ecumenical conversations on the global level have sought a clearer understanding of the sacramental presence of Christ "in bread and wine."

In this process, two misplaced concentrations have been increasingly edged out of the picture:

1. The concentration on "the elements" in themselves — without a perspective on the event of the meal as a whole or on the personal presence of Christ.

2. The concentration on an abstract "ubiquity" of Christ — without clear perspectives on word, sacrament, and Christ's personal and real presence.

The element of truth contained in the notion of the ubiquity of Christ is grasped when we recognize that when the risen Christ is present in the Supper, so is the exalted Christ. With him the entire life of the pre-Easter Jesus is present. This life is not present in the elements in themselves, but in the elements of the Supper, in which a twofold process of reconciliation takes place, in which human beings, focused on the self-giving of Jesus Christ: (a) praise God and carry out a communal process of giving and taking, eating and drinking; (b) celebrate reconciliation with God and reconciliation of human beings with each other.

In this process the whole Christ is present: the pre-Easter Jesus whom we remember, the Crucified One whom we proclaim, the Risen One to whom we bear witness, and the Human One whom we expect and await. In the celebration of the Supper, the gathered community is permeated and surrounded by Christ, by the entire richness of his life. The notion of Christ's "real presence" is better suited than that of Christ's personal presence to provide a framework for the difficult task of understanding this complex of relations.

CHAPTER 6

"As Often as You Eat This Bread and Drink the Cup, You Proclaim Christ's Death . . ."

What Is Revealed by the Proclamation of Christ's Cross in the Celebration of the Supper?

What happens in holy communion? The sixth answer is: *In the center of the Supper's celebration stands a situation of abysmal guilt and suffering, and the liberating and joyful overcoming of that guilt and suffering. With the proclamation of Christ's death, the Supper renders the power of sin present. The Supper proclaims Christ's sacrifice in his self-giving abandonment to the powers of this world. It renders present Christ's victimization at the hands of human beings. It celebrates the (atoning) liberation of human beings from sin as guilt and as power that enslaves them.*

"As often as you eat this bread and drink the cup, you proclaim the Lord's death until he comes." Naturally this statement of 1 Corinthians 11:26 is cited over and over again in numerous twentieth-century ecumenical conversations and consensus texts on holy communion. At the same time, this statement remains remarkably isolated and obscure in the actual discussions of the theology of the Supper. As a rule it is quoted only to make the connection with reflections on Christ's coming and on the life of the community in eschatological hope, awaiting and expecting his coming. But in the reflections and consultations of churches on the global level, the proclamation of death remains just as strikingly omitted — apart from occasional reflections on the theme of "sacrifice/offering" — as the phrase "in the night in which he was betrayed" (see chapter 2) and the significance of the theme of "sin" (see chapter 10). What does it mean to say: You proclaim, as often as you eat this bread and drink the cup, the death of Christ? Why does the community proclaim Christ's death, when the community celebrates the presence of the risen and exalted Christ? What does it mean to proclaim death at all? We must now confront these difficult questions.

Can the "Real Presence" of Jesus Christ in the Supper Be Separated from the "Real Presence" of His Self-Giving Death on the Cross?

The "real presence" of Jesus Christ in the Supper is not to be separated from the "real presence" of his self-giving and death on the cross. All good, joyful, and liberating observations, impressions, experiences, and statements —

- about his being in the rich blessings bestowed in the gifts of creation;
- about his presence in the unity of the reconciliation of human beings with God and the reconciliation of human beings with each other;
- about his personal presence in the liturgical meal of peace and of God's glorification;
- about the vital joy, growing out of Christ's presence in the Supper, that is accessible to sense experience;
- about the riches of Christ's presence in the power of the resurrection;

— all these good and happy impressions, insights, and statements, and many others like them, lose their power, indeed become false and deceitful, if they ignore Jesus' betrayal, the utter gift of his body and blood, and his cross and death.

It is admittedly understandable and correct that people have sought to prevent the good, happy, and liberating aspects and experiential impulses of the Supper from being suppressed and repressed in the name of "cross and sin." It is understandable that people engaged in polemics against "austerity, aridity, morbid thoughts, or a Good Friday mood"[1] when these

1. See note 4; but cf. Christian Möller, *"Wenn der Herr nicht das Haus baut . . .": Briefe an Kirchenälteste zum Gemeindeaufbau* (Göttingen: Vandenhoeck, 1993), p. 77: "Banning talk of the forgiveness of sins from the Supper introduces superficial cheerfulness and an intoxicated enthusiasm for 'community' into the celebration of the Supper."

threatened to imprint and to overshadow the entire celebration of the Sacrament. This book — not the least of whose sources is the experience of suffering through the "sad colloquy" of disoriented celebrations of the Supper (cf. the Introduction) — is only one of the many efforts to recognize and to remove theological and liturgical errors that led and continue to lead to the distortion and obfuscation of good, happy, and liberating aspects of the celebration of the Supper. But all these justified efforts cannot and must not in turn distort and obscure the fact that the center of the Supper refers us to Jesus' suffering and dying, and to the significance of his death for "his own" and for the world.

Of course, the presence of the Crucified One does not exhaust the personal and real presence of Christ. But without the former, the latter cannot be conceived. Indeed, it is not only the case that the fullness of Christ's presence necessarily includes his death and the identity of the Crucified. The fullness of Christ's presence in the Supper concentrates precisely

- on the broken, torn, divided, utterly given bread;
- on the symbol of the shed blood, which burdens and horrifies many people;
- on the "night of betrayal" and the threatening presence of betrayers;
- on the memory of powerlessness, guilt, brutality, and crime;
- on the cross of Christ with all its burdensome significations;
- on an abyss of death and mourning, guilt and shame, seriousness and horror.

To be sure, it is not the point of the Supper to weigh people down, desensitize them, and to drive them to apathy, self-doubt, and self-torment. We cannot simply accept it when the Supper is so lamentably misused, when the Supper appears to be — or actually has the effect of — not a meal of reconciliation, liberation, and peace, but a source of religious and moral burdens and afflictions, a source of neurotic and self-tormenting attitudes. We must summon all our theological, pastoral, and ecclesially critical powers against such misuse! But this does not happen by holding in contempt and as much as possible ignoring all aspects of the Supper that one way or another come across as serious or burdensome. To be sure, we can make the attempt to "amputate" all elements of the Supper that one way or another come across as serious and burdensome, and to celebrate a religious and sociable ritual that spares people the confrontation with betrayal, utter self-giving, guilt, cross, and death. But it then should be very clear that here it is no longer Christ's Supper that we are celebrating. It should be made clear that reconciliation, liberation, joy, and peace in their seriousness and depth remain out of reach of those who celebrate such a ritual. It should be made clear that human beings are thereby cheated out of the sacramental presence of Christ.

The Proclamation of Christ's Death as Proclamation of His Cross

At the center of holy communion stands the liberating, joy-giving overcoming of a situation of abysmal guilt and suffering. But this means that the situation of abysmal guilt and suffering itself also stands at the center of holy communion. Not only the "night of betrayal," but also the cross and death of Jesus Christ stand at the center of the Supper. Christ's cross and death are brought before our eyes in public proclamation as often as the Supper is celebrated. For those engaged in the celebration of the Supper, as well as beyond that circle, that celebration "proclaims the Lord's death." That death is publicly proclaimed and made known. Well may we rush to add the following caveats:

- Christ's death is proclaimed in such a way that human beings experience a great liberation;
- Christ's death is proclaimed in such a way that people recognize therein the basis of their reconciliation with God and with each other;
- Christ's death is proclaimed in such a way that people are moved to remember Jesus Christ with grateful hearts and to give thanks and glory to God.

But even when we immediately add these and other caveats and give reasons for them, the fact of the "proclaimed death of the Lord" still stands at the center of the Supper.

It is therefore with good reason that many liturgies of holy communion provide for the *Agnus Dei.* In connection with John 1:29 ("The next day he [John the Baptist] saw Jesus coming toward him and declared, 'Here is the Lamb of God who takes away the sin of the world!'"), the *Agnus Dei* was introduced into the Roman mass prior to A.D. 700: "O Christ, thou Lamb of God, that takest away the sin of the world, have mercy upon us." The period between the ninth and eleventh centuries saw the development of the threefold repetition and most likely the conclusion to the third repetition: "Grant us thy peace."

The proclamation of Christ's death takes seriously and meditates upon that which every person sees who opens the door of a Christian church: the cross of Christ. This cross stands for the potentiation of the "night of betrayal" to the public triumph of betrayal. The cross stands for the fact that Jesus of Nazareth, who proclaimed the coming reign of God and who freed many people from sickness and possession, was apparently shown to be in the wrong, condemned, and exposed to contempt. The cross stands for the fact that, by virtue of what happened to Jesus of Nazareth, the God whom Jesus proclaimed and whom he called "my Father" was called into question at the most basic level: "My God, my God, why have you forsaken me?"

But the cross does not stand for just any process by which Jesus, the God whom he proclaimed, and Jesus' communion with that God might be called into question. The cross stands for the fact that Jesus of Nazareth was condemned to a shameful and torturous death and was executed

- in the name of religion,
- in the name of the ruling politics,
- in the name of two legal systems (Roman and Jewish),
- with the support of public opinion ("All of them said, 'Let him be crucified!'").

The cross confronts us with the hideous knowledge that religion, law, politics, morality, and public opinion — all of them institutions that arc supposed to serve piety, public order, universal justice, and the promotion of human community and of what is good — can collaborate in driving the human beings who use these institutions into ongoing falsehood, injustice, mercilessness, disintegration, and distance from God. The abysmal power of the systematic masking and reinforcement of relations detrimental to life — the power that the biblical traditions call "sin" — becomes manifest "under the cross."

The situation that becomes manifest is one that encounters us in an obvious way when we look back — or from the outside — at societies and epochs fundamentally corrupted by fascism, racism, ecological brutality, or in other ways. But it is a situation which, even in those times and places where it is not obvious in the world, is latent. It is a situation of systematic and systemic corruption, in which the religious, political, judicial, moral, and other forces of reciprocal normative control and correction are absent as a whole. According to the testimony of the biblical traditions, natives and foreigners, the occupied and the forces of occupation, Jews and Romans, Jews and Gentiles collaborate in Jesus' crucifixion. That is, the entire representative world cooperates and conspires here against God's presence and against the powers of life. The "back-up controls" exercised by a global public, another judicial order, another religion, or even "the enemy" are absent here. Here it is not just the elites, but the gathered "crowd" (the concrete public), and even Jesus' most intimate circle, who collaborate together.

The Cross as Revelation of the Sin and Lostness of the World, and of the Suffering of God

The cross of Christ places before our eyes the unsurpassable depths of the human power for destruction and self-destruction. The cross confronts us with chaos and horror. It confronts us with the fact that religion and law, politics and morality, memory and public opinion are fundamentally corruptible and corrupt. It confronts human beings with our abysmal power to spread destruction, meaninglessness, and hopelessness. With "the Lord's death," this is proclaimed and made public in the celebration of the Supper. The celebration of the Supper does not pass over the cross in silence or try to bury it in secrecy. It does not trivialize or explain away the death of Christ. On the contrary, it uncovers a horrible event: on the cross, the failure of an entire world becomes manifest. Religion, law, politics, and public opinion — but also neighbors, friends, and disciples — turn against the one who proclaimed in word and deed God's presence, God's righteousness, and God's love. In part they turn against him with evil intent; in part they turn helplessly away. All this is proclaimed "with the Lord's death."

The proclamation of Christ's cross, indeed of his death, pulls the rug out from under all religious, legal, political, and moral self-righteousness of human beings. In the light of this proclamation no one can boast, no one can point the finger at others, can separate oneself from others, can elevate and look down on others. All illusions are destroyed that human beings can by their own power deliver and liberate themselves from their own act of closing themselves off from God. The self-inflicted condition of being closed off from God, the self-encapsulation against the powers of

Good, against justice, against what is creative, against life — this is what the biblical traditions call *sin.*[2] The proclamation of Christ's cross brings before our eyes a situation of "the sin of the world" in which all fuses are blown, all immune systems have failed, and God alone can help.

Yet how can God help in this situation, if — and this is what is most terrifying about the cross of Christ — the entire representative world — all powers, all agents responsible for order — have conspired in a "will to be far from God" (H.-G. Geyer)? How can God help, if the world so to speak hermetically seals itself off from God, if the world can completely cut itself loose from God and can set itself in opposition to God? In the cross we must consider and endure the possibility and the reality that God no longer has access to the world. On the cross looms the specter of failure for God's will to reveal himself through Jesus of Nazareth, through Jesus' proclamation of the coming reign of God, and through Jesus' actions. God's intentions to reveal himself in unrestrained love for human beings and in unrestrained solidarity with them are in danger of going unfulfilled. God's gift of self in the incarnation, in the entrance into the relations of human life, goes unrecognized. The cross confronts God with the death and sin of the world in a way that calls into question not only Jesus' life, but the divine life.

What kind of God is this, whose will for revelation runs up against limits? What kind of God is this, who while desiring the greatest intimacy with human beings ends up at the greatest distance from them? The cross calls God most profoundly, most abysmally into question. The direct confrontation with sin and death profanes the most holy God. The creator God is confronted with the chaos that calls creation into question. The revelation of the divine love in Jesus Christ comes to grief in the face of organized hatred and organized power. Although the powers by which God wills to rule the world are actually good, they become completely perverted and corrupted. The cross reveals a suffering of God, a powerlessness of God — not only the suffering and death of Jesus Christ, but suffering and powerlessness in the depths of the Godhead.

In this powerlessness of God, as it becomes manifest on the cross, we recognize two things. We recognize the communion of the Creator, the Holy Spirit, and the crucified Jesus over against a world that shuts God out (see especially chapter 12). But we also recognize a divinity of which

2. See Sigrid Brandt, Marjorie Suchocki, and Michael Welker, eds., *Sünde: Ein unverständlich gewordenes Thema* (Neukirchen-Vluyn: Neukirchener, 1997).

it is now really true that nothing human is foreign to it, a divinity that has given itself over to the abyss of human misery and horror. We recognize a God who has exposed himself not only to death, but to the abysmal distance from God which some biblical traditions call "hell." Whatever the character of the conceptions connected with the expression, the tradition has used the language of Jesus' descent into hell to express this state of affairs. (By contrast, the phrase "descended into the realm of the dead" trivializes this confrontation of God with hell.) We can articulate this state of affairs in the sentence: On the cross hell becomes manifest. But it also becomes manifest that hell is not foreign to God, that God suffers hell, that God exposes the divine life to this suffering.

However, the proclamation of "the Lord's death" in the celebration of holy communion, the public declaration of the world's lostness and of the night of abandonment by God point at the same time to God's power, which alone has helped and which alone can help. According to the Easter message, the presence of the risen Christ has freed human beings from this situation of complete hopelessness, a complete dead end. But it is not an otherworldly, numinous savior figure who meets us in the risen Christ. In the risen Christ we meet the one who, looking ahead in the "night of his betrayal," promises his presence in bread and wine, who institutes the communal meal "in his memory," and who ties his presence and God's creative powers into this meal.

The celebration of the Supper takes the situation of the cross, a situation of abysmal guilt and suffering, and reveals and proclaims it as a situation that Jesus has already mercifully anticipated and overcome. The remembrance of the pre-Easter Jesus, who institutes the Supper so that in all times, even in times of greatest distress, his disciples can ensure themselves of their communion with him and can renew this communion, recognizes in this pre-Easter Jesus the Christ of the resurrection. The experience of the presence of the risen Christ blossoms in the remembrance of Jesus who, beset on all sides in the "night of betrayal," in the midst of unfaithful or at least helpless disciples, looks ahead with love and care for the welfare of others. In the light of Jesus' faithfulness, the cross and death are remembered and proclaimed. The evil and helplessness of the world and the "night of God-forsakenness" are made present in the light of God's faithfulness and love.

Supper and Sacrifice: A Tangled Web of Problems Must Be Untangled

Jesus' faithfulness and love can hardly be questioned, even by those persons who have only passing acquaintance with his person and his life. By contrast, talk of God's faithfulness and love in connection with the cross of Christ has most decidedly become questionable and offensive for many people. This is bound up not only with unclear notions of God's passionate love for human beings, as that love becomes manifest on the cross. First and foremost, it stems from the in part unclear, in part false conceptions of "Jesus' sacrifice on the cross" and of the "atonement" wrought by that "sacrifice."

The false conception says that the cross of Christ not only reveals the abysmal sin of humanity, but also shows that a "just" God requires a *compensation* for human beings' deficiency. Since no sinful human being is in a position to produce this "atoning" compensation, the sinless Son of God, the Lamb of God, must be sacrificed. Only this sacrifice can pacify God's anger. Such ideas have functioned in our cultures as a background paradigm to entrench and to idealize a turn of mind radically conformed to models of judicial and economic compensation. Compensation comprises the ultimate cultural background, the basis of normativity, the ethical center, the hard core of religion. This has propagated a latent image of God that is deeply unchristian, indeed demonic: This God is always seeking compensation; it takes a sacrificial victim to calm and pacify this ultimately merciless and vengeful God, to satisfy the divine interest in compensation. And it must be a living sacrifice, a bloody and innocent sacrifice. Without such a sacrifice this God cannot be pacified. Great theological and exegetical exertions were necessary to liberate the theology of the cross and holy communion from these background ideas which are nothing less than destructive of faith.

The ecumenical conversations in the last decades of the twentieth century concerning holy communion have done little to explore and clarify the relation between the Supper and Jesus' "sacrifice" on the cross in terms of christological content.[3] Nevertheless, they have made clear that

3. Cf. the critique in Eckhard Lessing, *Abendmahl,* Bensheimer Ökumenische Studienhefte 1 (Göttingen: Vandenhoeck, 1993), pp. 60ff., 80ff., 110ff. See also David Power, "Words That Crack: The Uses of 'Sacrifice' in Eucharistic Discourse," in R. Kevin

the celebration of the Supper does not call into question the uniqueness and one-time nature of Jesus' sacrifice on the cross.[4] To a large extent, the door has been closed on the objection, so often repeated from the Protestant side, that the Catholic "sacrifice of the mass" intends to repeat in the eucharist the sacrifice of Christ on the cross.

The fateful concept of the "compensatory sacrifice of atonement" has been subjected to a radical critique by the theological discussion outside of the process of ecumenical agreement. But in the consensus texts we find only a few places that attempt to develop a constructive understanding of "sacrifice" that corresponds to the New Testament texts. In opposition to the false understanding presented above, the 1977 final report of the World Alliance of Reformed Churches and the Secretariat for Promoting Christian Unity, "The Presence of Christ in Church and World," offers substantial statements on the theme "the sacrifice of Jesus Christ" — along with some efforts to clarify the relation between "sacrifice" and "remembrance."

> The sacrifice brought by Jesus Christ is his obedient life and death (cf. Heb 10:5-10; Phil 2:8). His once-for-all self-offering under Pontius Pilate is continued by him forever in the presence of the Father in virtue of his resurrection. . . . In its joyful prayer of thanksgiving, "in the Eucharist," when the Church of Christ remembers his reconciling death for our sins and for the sins of the whole world, Christ himself is present, who "gave himself up on our behalf as an offering and sacrifice whose fragrance is pleasing to God" (Eph 5:2). Sanctified by his

---

Seasoltz, ed., *Living Bread, Saving Cup: Readings on the Eucharist* (Collegeville, Minn.: Liturgical Press, 1987), pp. 157ff.

4. "The Eucharist" 1978 [L-RC], p. 205. Cf. "Dublin Report" 1976 [M-RC], p. 354: "Roman Catholics . . . see the eucharist not as another sacrifice adding something to Christ's once-for-all sacrifice, not as a repetition of it, but as making present in a sacramental way the same sacrifice. For some Methodists such language would imply that Christ is still being sacrificed." "The Eucharist" 1978 [L-RC], p. 207: "According to Catholic doctrine the sacrifice of the Mass is the making present of the sacrifice of the cross. It is not a repetition of this sacrifice and adds nothing to its saving significance. When thus understood, the sacrifice of the Mass is an affirmation and not a questioning of the uniqueness and full value of Christ's sacrifice on the cross." "Eucharistic Doctrine: Elucidation" 1979 [A-RC], p. 74: "The Church in celebrating the eucharist gives thanks for the gift of Christ's sacrifice and identifies itself with the will of Christ who has offered himself to the Father on behalf of all mankind."

Spirit, the Church — through, with, and in God's Son, Jesus Christ — offers itself to the Father. It thereby becomes a living sacrifice of thanksgiving, through which God is publicly praised (cf. Rom 12:1; 1 Pet 2:5).[5]

However, without further clarifications, the talk of Christ's "offering" continues to prove susceptible to encouraging a conception of a God who requires compensation for the "sin of the world," and to that end causes "innocent blood" to flow. This conception has been operative for centuries, with devastating consequences. But now to a large extent a comprehensive undertaking of theological research and discussion has cleared it up and removed it from the picture.

1. "Atonement" Is a Salvific Event (H. Gese, B. Janowski)

As Hartmut Gese first showed in his pathbreaking essay "The Atonement,"[6] atonement engages human life, bringing help, healing, and salvation, at the point where life has been forfeited. Atonement engages life where human beings — even with their best medical, judicial, and other means — cannot undo the fact that they have fallen prey to death, that their lives are shot through with insecurity. Atonement engages life where the human person stands in an "irreparable process of disintegration — irreparable because it includes the boundaries of her existence. The human person stands in the situation where nothing can be made good again." Atonement responds to the question: "When a human being, in whatever way, guiltily reaches the limits of her existence, or when a people finds itself in the corresponding situation, do they have the possibility of freeing themselves from this entrapment? Do they have the possibility of new life beyond the irreparable process?"[7]

5. "The Presence of Christ" 1977 [R-RC], p. 452.

6. Hartmut Gese, "Die Sühne," in *Zur biblischen Theologie: Alttestamentliche Vorträge,* Beiträge zur evangelischen Theologie 78 (Munich: Chr. Kaiser, 1977), pp. 85-106. Bernd Janowski was the first to expand on and futher develop Gese's insights. He was then followed by numerous New Testament scholars and systematic theologians. See esp. Bernd Janowski, *Sühne als Heilsgeschehen: Studien zur Sühnetheologie der Priesterschrift und zur Wurzel KPR im Alten Orient und im Alten Testament,* Wissenschaftliche Monographien zum Alten und Neuen Testament 55 (Neukirchen-Vluyn: Neukirchener, 1982), pp. 1ff., esp. 183ff.

7. Gese, "Sühne," pp. 86, 87.

Atonement is not reconciliation in the sense of pacifying God. Atonement takes place precisely in a situation where human beings have squandered all possibilities to achieve reconciliation with God. Only an incorrect understanding of atonement starts from the assumption that human beings, in their condition of having fallen prey to death, can achieve reconciliation with God: for example, by means of sacrifice. This assumption fails to recognize the seriousness of the accursed situation into which human beings have fallen, the situation in which they have squandered all possibilities. Human beings in the fateful nexus of sin and malignity, in the sphere of the curse, can only plunge deeper into their ill-fated existence with their own attempts to be reconciled to God. If an attempt to be reconciled to God were to meet with success, it would not lie within the sphere of the curse. The false idea of atonement has not clearly grasped the problematic of sin and of having fallen prey to sin. By contrast, as B. Janowski has put it, atonement is "the dissolution of the fateful nexus of sin and malignity. This dissolution is made possible by God, and in the cultic event of sacrifice it becomes reality for the benefit of human beings."[8] But how does God in Jesus Christ dissolve the fateful nexus of sin and malignity?

2. "Sacrifice" Is Always the Donation of Vital Resources, but Not Necessarily "Victimization" (S. Brandt)

In what way did Jesus "offer himself as a sacrifice"? In what way was his "sacrifice" brought before God? In another pathbreaking work, this time on the theme of sacrifice, Sigrid Brandt has continued and advanced the theological trajectory proceeding from the insights into "atonement" presented above.[9] She highlights a distinction that German and some other languages, unlike English, unfortunately do not make explicit. The German word *Opfer* can be translated into English as both "sacrifice" and "victim." On the one hand, we speak of a cultic "sacrifice" in the temple, or of the "sacrifice" that parents without means make for the education of

8. Janowski, *Sühne als Heilsgeschehen,* p. 359.

9. Sigrid Brandt, *Opfer als Gedächtnis: Zu einem evangelischen Verständnis von Opfer* (Münster: Lit, 2000), and bibliography. See also the excellent discussion in Paul Empie and T. Austin Murphy, eds., *The Eucharist as Sacrifice: Lutherans and Catholics in Dialogue III* (Minneapolis: Augsburg, n.d.), pp. 7ff.

their children. On the other hand, we speak of "victims" of a traffic accident, "victims" of drugs, "victims" of war. German and other languages like it must use the same word to cover both sets of cases. Many sacrifices claim to need a victim. But not every sacrifice is necessarily tied to victimization. And by no means is it permissible to religiously cloud the issue of victimization by treating victims as "sacrifices." Many instances of victimization attempt deceitfully to consecrate the destruction or killing of human beings by playing with the language of "sacrifice":

- The victims of war must be "offered" so that the people can live.
- The many traffic victims must be "sacrificed" to the great good of automobile culture and individual transportation.
- The victims of drugs must be "accepted" as dictated by the destiny of certain cultures or by the misuse of individual freedom.

In precisely this sense, we can mask Jesus' victimization on the cross by saying that God willed that Jesus be victimized.

In opposition to such ideological and religious masking strategies, Brandt shows that the incarnation of Jesus Christ is a sacrifice in the sense that, in the incarnation, God "gives" himself to the world of human beings. The divine life becomes subject to confusion with earthly life; the divine life becomes vulnerable. In this sense, the divine life is "given" as a sacrifice. But this does not mean that God willed — or even planned and intended! — the victimization of Jesus on the cross at the hands of human beings. However, this reprehensible victimization does not prevent God from keeping faith with human beings! God does not will the victimization of Jesus. But God does not permit the fact that human beings and the powers of this world make a victim of Jesus to ruin Jesus' sacrifice and God's care for human beings.

When in the celebration of holy communion we think of "Christ's sacrifice," we should distinguish between:

- the grateful remembrance of Christ's sacrificial gift of love and faithfulness, and of God's love and faithfulness, which refuse to let the guilt of human beings prevent God from remaining among human beings, entering into connection with them, and acting creatively in and among them; and
- the consciousness of the guilt and lostness of human beings and of the world, which put Christ on the cross as a victim.

The language of sacrifice articulates the fact that God gives up all divine power, that God engages the creaturely on its own terms, with its forces and powers, that God gives the world room for its own development, with the attendant costs and consequences for God. God desires to demonstrate the divine glory precisely in self-giving to us and to persons of other times and regions of the world, precisely in the breadth and depth of this self-giving. Admittedly, the notion of "self-giving" has been so strongly misused — for example, in sexist or militaristic ways — that it has become an unfortunate or at least highly problematic concept. Perhaps we need new ways of talking that would enable us to distinguish the glossed over oppression, subjugation, and "offering up" of human beings from free and creative self-engagement and self-giving for others. Perhaps the clear distinction between sacrifice and victim, between sacrificial offering and victimization, offers a way out of the fateful consequences of the linguistic confusion both inside and outside religion.

The celebration of holy communion, rightly understood, can be helpful in this urgently required process of insight and renewal. A meal of peace takes up within itself the remembrance of the cross and the proclamation of Christ's death. A symbolic meal of gratefully glorifying God, of mutually welcoming one another, and of experiencing joy with one another, includes the remembrance of God's loving self-giving, which is greater and more encompassing than all rejection of God and all worldly aggression against God. The Supper is not a suffocating and oppressive religious ritual, or a ritual of endangerment. Nor is it an occasion to remember a catastrophe with a terrible outcome. Even in the "proclamation of the Lord's death," the Supper remains a celebration of liberation and joy. The proclamation of Christ's death is and remains directed toward the coming of Christ and the coming of God's reign. The seriousness of memory in the proclamation of Christ's death is taken into the great and joyfully hopeful expectation of the deliverance of the world through Christ's becoming completely present.

Results

The "real presence" of Jesus Christ in holy communion cannot be separated from the "real presence" of his self-giving and death on the cross. A situation of abyssal guilt and suffering is at the center of the celebration of the Supper. The cross stands for the potentiation of the "night of betrayal" to the public triumph of betrayal. The cross stands for the fact that Jesus of Nazareth is condemned to a shameful and torturous death and executed in the name of religion, in the name of the dominant politics, in the name of a twofold law, and supported by public opinion. The cross reveals a situation in which the confrontation with sin, death, and chaos call God profoundly into question.

But in looking back to the institution of the Supper and in light of the resurrection, the cross also reveals that Jesus has already mercifully anticipated and overcome the situation of abyssal guilt and suffering. By instituting the Supper, Jesus makes it possible for his disciples to renew communion with him at all times, even in times of greatest distress. This renewal of communion with God is to be understood as "atonement," for atonement opens up new life in the midst of an "irreparable process."

Jesus Christ's entire self-giving, God's favor to human beings in Jesus Christ, is also to be seen as "sacrifice" (self-giving and donation of life). Here we must clearly distinguish sacrifice from victimization. Even in the face of victimization by human beings, Jesus Christ maintains his faithful self-giving, his readiness to put his life on the line for human beings. In this light we must reject the false understanding of atonement which says that God plans and wills the victimization of Jesus in order to satisfy the divine need for vengeance and compensation.

CHAPTER 7

You Proclaim Christ's Death "Until He Comes"

The Hope for the Complete Revelation of God in the Whole Creation

The seventh answer to the question "What happens in holy communion?" is: *The death of Jesus Christ is proclaimed until his so-called coming, until his so-called return, until his "parousia" (1 Cor 11:26). Christ's cross and Christ's death are proclaimed in the celebration of the Supper until the complete presence of Jesus Christ in the entire creation. In this way the power of sin over the world is recognized. It becomes clear that the world is unconditionally dependent on God's saving action.*

Why We Have Trouble Imagining Christ's "Coming"

The talk of the "coming" or "return" of Jesus Christ is misleading inasmuch as for some people it creates the impression that the pre-Easter Jesus will appear again "at the end of time." Already in the Gospels one finds warnings against such conceptions: "And if anyone says to you at that time, 'Look! Here is the Messiah!' or 'Look! There he is!' — do not believe it" (Mk 13:21; Mt 24:23). Just as Jesus' resurrection is not the revivification of the pre-Easter Jesus, the so-called coming of Christ is not the renewed appearance of the human Jesus. For this reason it is more accurate to speak of Jesus Christ's *parousia,* of the onset of his reign, in order to designate the coming of Christ. Yet how are we to imagine the onset of Christ's reign?

The *parousia* of the crucified and risen Christ is a central part of the confession of faith in the Apostles' and Nicene Creeds. The exalted Christ, who sits at the right hand of the Father, will come out of heaven "to judge the living and the dead." But this conception causes extreme difficulties for modern persons and their consciousness of reality. They have similar problems with the New Testament images that the Human One will come on the clouds of heaven, that he will come with the angels, that he will send out his angels (for example, Mk 13), or that heaven and earth will flee before God's presence and that the sea, like death and the underworld, will give forth the dead (Rev 20). But it is also the case that modern persons hardly find plausible the hope that we will be redeemed from our bodies and just so will be "revealed as children of God" (Rom 8). Are not these all fantastic notions — in part terrifying fantasies, at best mere pipe dreams — that have lost all touch with reality?

On the basis of what we have so far come to understand about what happens in holy communion, we must also not evade this difficult theme of Christ's return. The celebration of the Supper takes place in communion with the past, present, and future church of Christ (see chapter 9 for a detailed discussion). The celebration of the Supper ties together in community the living and the dead and the not yet born. In this lively community, which necessarily transcends all our conceptions — it is a community not only in our time and world! — God's reign is "in advent," "in coming," and we are oriented toward the coming of Jesus Christ. The image of the complete and definitive *parousia* of Christ must be placed in relation to this broad community that necessarily transcends all earthly contexts of experience. Not only do "we, here and now," proclaim the Lord's death until he comes, but a multitude of other human beings and communities in distant bygone times have proclaimed and awaited his coming, and persons and communities in times and regions of the world that are completely removed from us will yet proclaim Christ's death in orientation toward his complete revelation.

The imagistic conceptions of the New Testament compel us consciously to break open our conceptions of world, reality, and future, to the extent that these conceptions are bound solely to our world, our reality, and our time. The New Testament conceptions compel us to grasp the onset of Christ's reign not in one particular time and world, but in all times and all worlds. The risen Christ refuses to be without "his own" and is not without them, not without his post-Easter body, not without his witnesses. Therefore the biblical texts speak of his coming with the elect and with the angels, who assemble not merely out of *one* particular time and region of the world, but out of all times and all regions of the world. According to the formulation of Mark 13, the Human One will bring together all the elect, and not only from one end of the earth to the other, but "from the ends of the earth to the ends of heaven" (Mk 13:27). The apocalyptic images of Revelation 20 adhere to similar ways of thinking. These images connect the glory of God and of the Lamb with the passing away of heaven and earth, and with the dissolution of finitude and death.

The biblical texts — like the talk of the *parousia* — speak of a hope that the glory of the resurrection will illumine all times and regions of the world. They speak of a hope in the presence of the exalted Christ — a hope that transcends all hopes which are tied to a specific finitude. They break through the egotism of the witnesses living in any particular time and place, including every "collective egotism," by virtue of the fact that their expectations include prior, subsequent, and contemporary times and worlds. They overcome the limited nature of particular expectations, wishes, and longings, without belittling them or jumping over them by means of fantastic speculations. The biblical texts speak of this world, these bodies, this heaven, and this earth passing away. Speaking in this way serves the clear logic and the material appropriateness of a trajectory of theological reflection that moves beyond every relative world. The liturgy of holy communion is even more realistic in its emphasis: Until the *parousia,* we proclaim the death of Christ. Until Christ is completely revealed, we see the world in the shadow of the cross.

With this orientation toward the complete presence of Christ in creation, we are able to see a perspective that critically takes up our hopes. We must move beyond the practice of absolutizing *our* world; we must move beyond absolutizing conceptions and generalizations that simply reproduce and extend that world. Our hopes, expectations, and conceptions must not overlay and obscure the wealth of images and expectations of Christ, the wealth of hopes for Christ's advent and the advent of God's reign — including the images, expectations, and hopes of past and future Christians and Christian communities. We must take seriously and accept the wealth, the diversity, and the inexhaustibility of times and worlds, without losing sight of their shared concentration on Christ's *parousia.*

The Lordship of Jesus Christ and the Reign of God Are "in Advent"

The proclamation of Christ's death in the celebration of the Supper is directed toward Christ's coming. This coming corresponds to the coming of the reign of God, for which we pray in the Lord's Prayer: "Your kingdom come." Concerning this reign of God and its advent we read: "Nor will they say, 'Look, here it is!' or 'There it is!' For, in fact, the reign of God is (already) among you" (Lk 17:21). The advent of the reign of God can indeed be experienced in the spread of love, mercy, forgiveness, and true justice. But the reign of God cannot be "nailed down." It is not wrapped up and delivered as a whole package, so that we could take possession of it. Exactly the same thing is true of the coming Christ, the coming Human One. To be sure, Christ is present with his witnesses, in their proclamation, in their deeds of love in his name, in the celebration of holy communion. But no witness, no time and culture, no church, and no ecclesial or religious movement, no matter how successful, possesses, has, or controls the coming Christ. They all stand in the movement of proclamation, which is directed toward his full entry in sovereignty, the full revelation of his presence in creation.

In spite of the presence of the fullness of Christ in the "real presence," the fact that the celebration of the Supper is directed toward the coming of Christ requires us to respect the liveliness of Christ and to take seriously the fact that Christ's presence does not fully encompass his future. However, this openness to the future of Christ does not turn the experience of his presence into something "temporary" in a bad and imperfect sense. Even if Christ's future is not yet completed, we have in his presence salvation in its entirety and complete comfort and encouragement. The recognition of the "fullness" of Christ in the real presence allows us to think about the dynamic relationships between his presence and his coming. Just as the whole Christ is present prior to Easter, although his life and his history with the world are not yet completed, so the whole Christ is also present for us in the celebration of the Supper, although we await his further delivering and revealing action toward creation.

This full experience of salvation while simultaneously living in expectation is formulated in the "Windsor Statement" of 1971:

> In the eucharist we proclaim the Lord's death until he comes. Receiving a foretaste of the kingdom to come, we look back with

> thanksgiving to what Christ has done for us, we greet him present among us, we look forward to his final appearing in the fullness of his kingdom when "The Son also himself (shall) be subject unto him that put all things under him, that God may be all in all" (1 Cor 15:28). When we gather around the same table in this communal meal at the invitation of the same Lord and when we "partake of the one loaf," we are one in commitment not only to Christ and to one another, but also to the mission of the church in the world.[1]

The 1978 document "The Eucharist" emphasizes that all dimensions of "salvation history" are included in this fullness of the presence of the coming Christ: The remembrance of the good creation, the breaking in of the "reality of sin," the "consolation and promise of God's word," bread and wine as gifts of creation, and the "basic features of human life" are all internally interconnected with the "union of Christians with their Lord and with each other . . . [as] the proclamation and the beginning of God's kingdom in our midst and a promise of the coming fulfilment."[2]

On this basis the living identity of the coming Christ can be perceived, recognized, and attested in the most diverse situations of life and world. We can affirm both Christ's identity in situations of life and world which are partially or totally beyond the reach of this time and world, and the continuing power of his activity in the many features of his person that have been manifest since before Easter. It is only in orientation toward the eschatological "coming of Jesus Christ" that we can grasp the continuing activity and the continuing vitality of Christ in faithfulness to himself and to his mission, and in faithfulness to the world — to "all the world" and to "this world of ours"! (cf. chapters 8 and 9). If the tradition has spoken of Christ's activity "in heaven," of his "advocacy before God," of his "heavenly intercession for us," etc., what it had in mind was this faithfulness of the living Christ to himself, which is at the same time the ground of his faithfulness to us and to our time and world, and the ground of our "preservation unto eternal life."

In the ecumenical conversations of the last decades of the twentieth century one can see that this unity of the killed and eternally living Christ, and his unity with "his own" — overarching all earthly distances and differences

1. "Windsor Statement" 1971 [A-RC], p. 69.

2. "The Eucharist" 1978 [L-RC], p. 194. The attendant perspectives of trinitarian theology also come into view on pp. 194ff. (see esp. chapter 12).

— must be conceived *pneumatologically:* that is, as mediated by the activity of the divine Spirit. In the words of the "Windsor Statement":

> The Lord who . . . comes to his people in the power of the Holy Spirit is the Lord of glory. In the eucharistic celebration we anticipate the joys of the age to come. By the transforming action of the Spirit of God, earthly bread and wine become the heavenly manna and the new wine, the eschatological banquet for the new man: elements of the first creation become pledges and first fruits of the new heaven and the new earth.[3]

This means that:

- in the power of the Holy Spirit Jesus Christ is the eternal Lord;
- in the power of the Holy Spirit the celebration of holy communion becomes an anticipation of eternal glory;
- by the power of the Holy Spirit the earthly gifts of bread and wine become heavenly gifts. From being gifts of creation, making temporal life possible, they become gifts of the new creation, giving eternal life.

Analogously to what is said about the coming Christ, we can also say concerning the Holy Spirit: "The presence of the Spirit is the foretaste, pledge, and first-fruits of God's coming Kingdom. At every Eucharist the Church looks forward to the consummation of that reign."[4]

The Supper as a "Meal of God's Reign" and as "Heavenly Liturgy"

Holy communion is directed toward the complete presence of Christ in the whole creation, and toward the fulfillment of the reign of God, toward its "having come completely." In this orientation, the Supper already participates in that to which it points. The church uses two images in its communion liturgies to express that toward which the Supper points, and in which it already participates: the "banquet of the reign of God" and the "heavenly liturgy."

3. "Windsor Statement" 1971 [A-RC], p. 71.
4. *God's Reign and Our Unity* 1984 [A-R], p. 43.

Set within the framework of the institution of the Supper, Matthew 26:29 reads: "I will never again drink of this fruit of the vine until that day when I drink it new with you in my Father's reign" (Mk 14:25: ". . . in the reign of God"; Lk 22:18: ". . . until the reign of God comes"). In Luke 22:16 Jesus says over the meal: "I will never eat it [the Passover meal] again until it is fulfilled in the reign of God." This fulfillment begins in the Supper. In the presence of the risen Christ, the banquet of the reign of God is celebrated. For in the presence of the risen Christ (which must not be limited to the celebration of the Supper), God's reign is "in advent," "in coming." The complete fulfillment of this reign and the complete *parousia* still lie before us. "Baptism, Eucharist and Ministry" describes this tension by saying that "the eucharist opens up the vision of the divine rule which has been promised as the final renewal of creation, and is a foretaste of it."[5]

Yet precisely this tension can be weighted differently: Inasmuch as the Supper is a foretaste, inasmuch as the shadow of the proclamation of Christ's death still lies over it (see especially chapters 2, 6, and 10), the Supper points to the path and the distance which lie between us and the fulfillment of God's rule. As long as this tension exists, this double perspective will continue to give rise to questions and differences: Should we already rejoice over the coming of Christ and of God's reign? Is the Supper in fact already a "banquet of the reign of God"? Or does it redirect our impatient expectation to that joyous banquet which still lies ahead of us? Should we wait impatiently for the heavenly meal, praying the *Maranatha:* "Our Lord, come!" (1 Cor 16:22) and the "Come, Lord Jesus!" with the appropriate passion?

It is first and foremost Orthodox theology that has repeatedly insisted that the faithful, through their participation in the Supper, "grow in that mystical divinization which makes them dwell in the Son and the Father, through the Spirit."[6] Orthodox theology has characterized this growth "in that mystical divinization" as participation in the heavenly doxology and in the heavenly liturgy. The church "celebrates the eucharist as expression here and now of the heavenly liturgy."[7] The ecumenical conver-

5. "Baptism, Eucharist and Ministry" 1982 [WCC], p. 479.

6. "The Mystery of the Church" 1982 [O-RC], p. 55. See Alexander Schmemann, *For the Life of the World: Sacraments and Orthodoxy* (Crestwood, N.Y.: St. Vladimir's Seminary Press, 1995).

7. "The Mystery of the Church" 1982 [O-RC], p. 55.

sations have emphasized with increasing clarity that precisely in the celebration of the Supper the Holy Spirit gathers, builds up, and sends the churches of all times and regions of the world, binding all these churches together in a way that far exceeds the capacity of our sense perception.

However, this uplifting and upbuilding is accompanied by a judgment on that life which is not in accordance with the being of Christ and the coming reign of God. To be sure, the Supper is not the place of this judgment, but inasmuch as it proclaims "the Lord's death," it registers the fact that the world closes itself to and refuses God's presence. For this reason many persons are not inordinately impatient in awaiting the end of this world, the fulfilled reign of God, and the complete presence of Christ. Instead they will happily accept God's merciful transformation of the world, God's activity toward and among them in their lifetime. They will happily accept the activity of God's Spirit toward and among them to prepare them for the complete presence of Christ. They will learn to appreciate the Supper as a meal on the way into the reign of God.

When our twin daughters were three years old they gave us a lovely example of how the impatient expectation of the fulfillment of the coming reign of God can switch to patience. Night after night before they went to sleep they wanted their mother to tell them something about "paradise." Their great-grandmother and other ancestors were in paradise. And the angels were there. And God. What does paradise look like? When are we going to paradise? How do we get there? What will we do there? There were questions on top of questions. One evening they wanted to know: "Mama, what is there to eat in paradise?" They picked up from my wife's answer that the "heavenly meal" did not correspond to their idea of "food." With a sigh of relief: "Well, we're still little!," the topic was over, permanently.

The celebration of the Supper proclaims Christ's death as long as the fullness of creatures, the fullness of times and worlds cannot join in the heavenly doxology before the face of God. The proclamation of Christ's death until the *parousia* and until the universal celebration of the Supper holds fast to the conviction that this heavenly praise of God, which already now is taking place, is *not* a fantastic conception of pie-in-the-sky. Instead it is a spiritual reality that is still "in advent," although it is already now exercising an influence in this world, reshaping, renewing, preserving, and transforming it. In the Lord's Prayer human beings ask for the coming of the reign of God, and this coming reign is already in effect in this orientation toward Christ's *parousia.* God's coming reign permeates our life realities with their various images of Christ, their various expectations of redemption, and their various hopes in God. In the celebration of the Supper human beings are taken into a community which is not an illusion or a fiction, although it calls into question every fixed conception of completion and perfection.

The proclamation of Christ's death until he comes corresponds to the hope that Paul formulates in 2 Corinthians 3:18: "All of us, with unveiled faces, seeing the glory of the Lord as though reflected in a mirror, are being transformed into the same image from glory to glory; for this comes from the Lord, the Spirit." God's glory is reflected by a community of those seized by God's Spirit, as this community continuously points beyond itself and grows beyond where it has been. Indeed, this community not only reflects God's glory, it embodies that glory in various forms — "from glory to glory" — in the rich fullness of the image of Christ, in the rich building up of Christ's body. But this goes hand in hand with the "proclamation of Christ's death" — with the recognition of the churches' position under the cross, with the recognition of Christ's sacrifice. This also goes hand in hand with the recognition that even our non-acceptance of the presence of the risen Christ and of his coming is always already surrounded by God, that Christ's self-giving and the Supper's celebration of that self-giving have always already anticipated our non-acceptance.

Results

In the celebration of the Supper the risen Christ of all times and all regions of the world is present. As long as the Supper is celebrated in a particular time and world and in a concrete community, we orient ourselves in expectation and hope toward the complete presence of Christ. On the one hand, we experience the world's imperfection, its condition of being threatened by the power of sin, and the still relative absence of Christ. On the other hand, we await the coming of the exalted Christ, his assumption of complete sovereignty. The New Testament's imagistic conceptions of Christ's *parousia* necessarily cause us difficulty, for they point toward a universality of the coming Christ which transcends all our conceptions of a perfected world history and a perfected future. The fact that Christ's *parousia* still lies ahead of us can, on the one hand, be experienced as a deficiency: We have only a pledge of the coming reign; we are still on the way to the banquet of God's reign and to the heavenly liturgy, in which the whole creation will glorify God. On the other hand, the same fact can find expression in rejoicing over Christ's vitality and his activity in the world — beyond all our imaginings. It can find expression in rejoicing that God is still at work on our world and on its merciful transformation, and that God's activity will redound not only to the benefit of future generations, but also to our benefit and that of past times and regions of the world.

CHAPTER 8

"Do This in Remembrance of Me"

Why the Supper Is Not Merely a Meal of Recollection: The Memory of Christ as Gift of the Holy Spirit and as Cultural Power

What happens in holy communion? The eighth answer is: *Holy communion is an event that establishes and confirms the remembrance of Jesus Christ. This "remembrance," this act of memory, includes firmly established and living memories, experiences, and expectations of the saving presence of Christ. It draws the human beings who establish and confirm this remembrance into the fullness of Christ's life. The remembrance of Christ is an effect of the Holy Spirit.*

Not Only: For Your Recollection of Me

The charge to celebrate the Supper "in remembrance" of Christ is found in Luke 22:19 and 1 Corinthians 11:24 and 25. This "act of remembrance," which in recent ecumenical conversations is also called the "memorial" or *anamnesis,* "means more than merely a mental act of 'recalling.'"[1] It signifies "much more than a bare act of intellectual remembrance of a past event." The remembrance is a "re-enactment of Christ's triumphant sacrifice and makes available for us its benefits."[2] The celebration of the Supper is not the mere individual and communal

1. "The Presence of Christ" 1977 [R-RC], p. 450.
2. "Denver Report" 1971 [M-RC], pp. 325, 326.

"internalization" of Christ's life, death, and resurrection. They are also and especially proclaimed and documented in a public way. The Supper sets up a living monument to them, so that the memory of Jesus Christ is carried further and spread abroad, and so that his remembrance is renewed and revitalized, concentrated and intensified.

This "remembrance" renders present "the totality of God's reconciling action" in the person of Christ:[3] "Christ himself with all that He has accomplished for us and for all creation (in his incarnation, servanthood, ministry, teaching, suffering, sacrifice, resurrection, ascension and Pentecost) is present in this *anamnesis* as is also the foretaste of his *Parousia* and the fulfilment of the Kingdom."[4] How can "the remembrance" do such great things?

"Collective Memory" as Cultural Power

"One tends to think of memory as a purely internal phenomenon, localized in the brain of the individual — a theme for neurophysiology, neurology, and psychology. . . . But what the content is that this memory absorbs, how it organizes this content, how long it is able to hold on to something, is in the broadest sense a question not only of internal capacity and direction, but also of overarching external conditions — that is, societal and cultural ones." In his important book *Cultural Memory*,[5] the German Egyptologist Jan Assmann — picking up on the work of Maurice Halbwachs,[6] Claude Lévi-Strauss,[7] and other theoreticians of the culture of memory — has provided a brilliant investigation of the cultural power of "memory." Memory is not only an individual or a communal mental phenomenon. It is, rather, a power for the communal generation of a world. Memory not only specifies to a high de-

3. Cf. "Ministry and Ordination" 1973 [A-RC], p. 82.

4. "The Eucharist" 1978 [L-RC], p. 196. A similar formulation is to be found in "Baptism, Eucharist and Ministry" 1982 [WCC], p. 477; cf. also *God's Reign and Our Unity* 1984 [A-R], p. 41.

5. Jan Assmann, *Das kulturelle Gedächtnis: Schrift, Erinnerung und politische Identität in frühen Hochkulturen* (Munich: Beck, 1992), pp. 19-20.

6. Maurice Halbwachs, *The Social Framework of Memory*, European Sociology Series (Ayer, 1975).

7. Claude Lévi-Strauss, *The Savage Mind* (Chicago: University of Chicago Press, 1966).

gree the common past, but also the shared present and the expected future. It creates cultural spaces which shape and mark human life no less than do natural spaces. The power of memory becomes clear when we observe the way in which "cultural memory" goes beyond the fluid "communicative memory."

A community's "communicative memory" is that shared memory which is continually being transformed. It is continually being enriched, and it is continually diminishing. In the course of each generation it shifts layers. Alongside this "communicative memory," which develops out of the concrete life circumstances of human societies, human beings develop a "cultural memory" that is as a rule long-lived. This cultural memory imposes meaning-bearing forms on their recollections (as well as on their actual experiences and their expectations). Only with difficulty can these forms be changed.[8] The cultural memory can work to stabilize a community against its own transformation (e.g., by means of the flow of communicative memory). The meaning-bearing forms of cultural memory can immunize human societies against being transformed. Lévi-Strauss called "cold societies" those societies that seek "to annul the possible effects of historical factors on their equilibrium and continuity."[9] Assmann speaks of "cold options of memory." But the cultural memory can also become a "hot memory," with which societies turn the remembered "historical process of becoming . . . into the motor of their development."[10]

However, the dynamizing "hot" memory and the stabilizing "cold" memory are not abstract alternatives. Highly developed human societies strive for a cultural memory that allows them to connect the continual stabilization of their identity and their dynamic development. As Assmann shows, the *canon* — for example, the biblical canon — is an institution that makes it possible for the cultural memory to achieve precisely that.[11] The canon stabilizes shared identity and requires living development in a wealth of individual and communal perspectives and interpretations. The canon makes possible the interplay of cold and hot

8. Cf. Assmann, *Das kulturelle Gedächtnis,* pp. 48ff.; Siegfried J. Schmidt, "Gedächtnis — Erzählen — Identität," in Aleida Assmann and Dietrich Harth, eds., *Mnemosyne: Formen und Funktionen der kulturellen Erinnerung* (Frankfurt: Fischer, 1991), pp. 378ff.

9. Lévi-Strauss, *The Savage Mind,* p. 234.

10. Assmann, *Das kulturelle Gedächtnis,* p. 75, following Lévi-Strauss.

11. Assmann, *Das kulturelle Gedächtnis,* pp. 103ff., esp. 126ff.

memory, thereby giving rise to a *living cultural memory* and putting it into effect.

Living cultural memory, canonical memory, is an astonishing power. On the one hand, a particular set of texts (e.g., the biblical traditions that grew up over a period of 1500 years) binds the cultural memory, imposing limits on its possibilities for transformation. On the other hand, the pluralistic manifold of perspectives contained in the canonical traditions stimulate a vitality of ongoing interpretation, which functions as hot cultural memory, but without consuming the basic historical resources and the shared identity.

The Living Cultural and Canonical Memory of Jesus Christ

The "memory of Christ," the memory which the celebration of holy communion renews and revitalizes, is one such living cultural or canonical memory. It reaches back to the three synoptic gospels (Matthew, Mark, Luke) with their in part highly similar, in part subtly differing presentations of Jesus' life and work, death and resurrection. It reaches back to the perspective of the Gospel of John and the very different perspectives of the New Testament epistolary literature, to the Acts of the Apostles, and to the Apocalypse. It is held in movement by the various "roles" of the earthly Jesus and by the various christological titles (Son of God, *Kyrios* or Lord, Human One, Messiah, etc.) with their particular spheres of recollection and expectation.

The living cultural or canonical memory connects a multitude of perspectives for rendering Jesus present, which are all related to each other in a continual interplay. In this canonical memory the risen Christ comes to the fore in the fullness of his person and of his pre-Easter history. The multitude of testimonies to the presence of the risen Jesus give rise to an unfolding of the fullness of life of the pre-Easter Jesus, of his utterances and intentions and, in all this, to a rich and lively recognition and glorification of his person and his continued effectiveness.

The accounts of the encounters with the risen Christ are excellent examples of the incendiary quality of canonical memory (see the Introduction). The breaking of bread, the perception of the wounds, the forms of address, and the "opening of the scriptures" give rise to the recognition of the presence of the risen Christ. One can imagine a multitude of further events that set the canonical memory in motion — from graciously turning attention to children and to sick, suffering, or possessed human beings, on the one hand, to the meal community's acceptance of the excluded, those placed under the stigma of taboo, violators of taboo, and collaborators, on the other hand.[12] Many events that would initiate canonical memory are also possible from Jesus' "symbolic political conflicts" with the temple cult and with the Roman Empire,[13] as well as from analogous conflicts in historically analogous constellations. Complex normative fields accrue to this canonical memory with Jesus' new interpretation of the law and his proclamation of the coming reign of God.[14] This and Jesus' claim to intimate communion with God the creator,[15] as well as his claim to the power to forgive sins, bring an explicitly religious dimension into the canonical memory, which indeed already has a religious quality in itself. The canonical memory has been and is able to proceed from these and other features of the historical Jesus and, in the interplay of fixed and fluid forms, to witness to the vitality of the presence of the risen Christ.[16]

The "memorial" that Jesus institutes by the celebration of the Supper makes the canonical memory based upon the biblical traditions focused, concrete, and existential. It weaves those who celebrate the Supper into the memory of Christ in a more basic way than is possible for interpretation and proclamation. The Emmaus disciples recognize the risen Christ in the breaking of the bread — only in hindsight does it become clear to them that their hearts were already burning within them while he was opening the scriptures to them!

12. Cf. John Dominic Crossan, *The Historical Jesus: The Life of a Mediterranean Jewish Peasant* (San Francisco: Harper, 1992), and *Jesus: A Revolutionary Biography* (San Francisco: Harper, 1995).

13. See G. Theissen, "Jesus und die symbolpolitischen Konflikte seiner Zeit: Sozialgeschichtliche Aspekte der Jesusforschung," *Evangelische Theologie* 57 (1997): 378-400.

14. Cf. M. Welker, "The Reign of God," *Theology Today* 49 (1992): 500-515.

15. See Eberhard Jüngel, *God as the Mystery of the World: On the Foundation of the Theology of the Crucified One in the Dispute between Theism and Atheism,* trans. Darrell L. Guder (Grand Rapids: Eerdmans, 1983), esp. pp. 343ff.; Wolfhart Pannenberg, *Systematic Theology,* vol. 2, trans. Geoffrey W. Bromiley (Grand Rapids: Eerdmans, 1994), pp. 363ff.

16. These various perspectives have certainly been capable of developing into one-sided and sometimes bizarre and ideological images of Jesus. But they have always been drawn back into the power of the living canonical memory, in which they were rendered problematic, recast, and renewed.

Called into the Remembrance of Christ

The ecumenical conversations on holy communion have accurately observed that in the "remembrance of Christ" revitalized and renewed by what happens in the Supper,

> more happens than that past events are brought to mind by this power of recall and imagination. The decisive point is not that what is past is called to mind, but that the Lord calls his people into his presence and confronts them with his salvation. In this creative act of God, the salvation event from the past becomes the offer of salvation for the present and the promise of salvation for the future.[17]

"Baptism, Eucharist and Ministry" calls the *anamnesis* "both representation and anticipation," "the church's effective proclamation of God's mighty acts and promises."[18]

This "temporal interlacing" in the "remembrance of Christ" is made fruitful in two more ways beyond what has already been presented. Inasmuch as Christ in the Supper gives the power "to live with him, to suffer with him and to pray through him as justified sinners," the "remembrance of Christ" is, on the one hand, "the basis and source of all Christian prayer. So our prayer relies upon and is united with the continual intercession of the risen Lord."[19] On the other hand, this process of being drawn into intercessory communion with Christ liberates us for a "reconciliation of memories."[20] This reconciliation of memories can serve as the soil from which grow both a sense for a new historical communion of the ecumenical churches, and an ecumenical peace that is able to absorb the pains and conflicts of the past and to stand firm in the face of further tests and burdens in the ecumenical pilgrim community.

The living canonical memory is a cultural power. The living canonical

17. "The Eucharist" 1978 [L-RC], pp. 200-201; cf. *Towards Closer Fellowship* 1987 [D-R], p. 8.

18. "Baptism, Eucharist and Ministry" 1982 [WCC], p. 477. In its response to BEM, the Church of England rightly speaks of the "total Christ-event from the creation by the Logos to the consummation of the Kingdom" (Max Thurian, ed., *Churches Respond to BEM: Official Responses to the "Baptism, Eucharist and Ministry" Text,* vol. 3, Faith and Order Paper 135 [Geneva: World Council of Churches, 1987], p. 44).

19. "Baptism, Eucharist and Ministry" 1982 [WCC], p. 477.

20. "Towards a Common Understanding" 1990 [R-RC], p. 224.

memory, in which the crucified and risen Jesus Christ can continually come anew to an effective presence, owes itself to the activity of God's Spirit, the Holy Spirit. The Holy Spirit is the power which continually renews the act of bringing human beings together for the solidification, renewal, revitalization, and enrichment of the memory of Christ. On the one hand, the Holy Spirit is the Spirit of Jesus Christ, through whom the risen Christ renders himself present among human beings. On the other hand, the Holy Spirit is the power that makes of human beings witnesses of Christ's presence, and gives them a share in Christ's life and creative vitality. The fact that the memory of Christ does not degenerate into a mere internal recollection or disintegrate into many internal recollections is to be ascribed to the activity of the Holy Spirit.[21] Therefore those who are celebrating the Supper pray for the presence of the Spirit, for the coming of the Spirit. In the recent ecumenical conversations it is above all the Orthodox churches that have repeatedly emphasized the significance of the invocation of the Spirit *(epiklesis)* (cf. chapters 11 and 12).

If we make clear to ourselves that the Holy Spirit makes it possible to raise up the memory of Christ, and that the Holy Spirit leads us to Christ and renders him present in our midst, we will then be able to recognize clearly that the memory of Christ is not something dreamed up and put together by human beings, although we most definitely participate in it and contribute to it. It will become clear that we human beings are called into this memory, in order to receive and to give a share in it. But the fact that this memory is effected by the Holy Spirit in no way means that it is something numinous. We can join with the theoreticians of the culture of memory to make clear outside the church as well that this memory is a cultural power that transforms the world.

Results

The celebration of the meal creates a memorial for Jesus Christ. Jesus' life, death, and resurrection are not simply internalized individually and com-

21. In its position statement on "Baptism, Eucharist and Ministry," the Presbyterian Church of Korea entered a plea for a clear connection between the christological and the pneumatological dimensions of the *anamnesis* (Max Thurian, ed., *Churches Respond to BEM: Official Responses to the "Baptism, Eucharist and Ministry" Text,* vol. 2, Faith and Order Paper 132 [Geneva: World Council of Churches, 1986], p. 162).

munally. They are publicly proclaimed, so that the memory of Christ is carried further and spread abroad. The memory of Christ is cultivated and spread as a living cultural memory, a canonical memory. This living cultural and canonical memory is at work in the midst of the fluid communicative memory that human societies continually vary, supplement, reconstruct, and re-layer (Jan Assmann). The living cultural and canonical memory imposes meaning-bearing forms on recollections, experiences, and expectations.

The memory concentrated on the presence of Jesus Christ grows out of interaction with the biblical traditions, especially those of the New Testament. In the celebration of the Supper this memory is bundled together in a concentrated way. Human beings are existentially bound into it and participate in its spread. Although human beings participate intensively in raising up the memory of Christ, this memory is not simply an achievement and accomplishment of human beings engaged in the process of recollection. It is a gift of the Holy Spirit, who calls and binds together the faithful, and makes it possible for Christ himself to act among them.

PART 3

Holy Communion — Feast of the Church of All Times and Regions of the World, Celebration of Peace and of the New Creation, and Joyful Glorification of the Triune God

CHAPTER 9

"Given for You" — "Shed for Many"

The Community Gathered Here and Now and the Ecumenical Church of All Times and Regions of the World

What happens in holy communion? The ninth answer is: *"The Supper is an act of worship of the community gathered in Jesus' name" (Arnoldshain Theses). At the same time, it is the feast of the church of all times and regions of the world.*

Deepest Certainty — Ecumenical Universality That Spans the Epochs

The Supper is the celebration of a symbolic meal of the concrete, gathered community (see especially chapter 1). Without calling this fact into question, we must supplement it by noting that the Supper is the celebration of the church of all times and all regions of the world. This interconnection becomes clear if we focus on the expressions: "Given for you!" and "Poured out for many!" The expression "poured out for many" is found in Matthew and Mark: "Then he took a cup, and after giving thanks he gave it to them, and all of them drank from it. He said to them, 'This is my blood of the covenant, which is poured out *for many*'" (Mk 14:24-25). Matthew 26:27 adds to the gift of the cup the invitation to drink from it: according to v. 28, the blood is poured out *for many* for the forgiveness of sins. Mark and Matthew already employ the phrase "for many" in the statement: "For the Human One came not to be served but to serve, and to give his life a ransom *for many*" (Mk 10:45; Mt 20:28). In contrast to the indeterminate expression "for many," in Luke we find for the bread as well as for the cup the determinate "given for you" and "poured out for you." First Corinthians 11:24 formulates the Supper tradition with the words: "This is my body that is for you."

The expressions "given for you" and "poured out for many" establish a double perspective on what is happening in holy communion. On the one hand, the addressee is the concrete, gathered community with its fundamental experiences in the celebration of the Supper: The symbolic actions of giving and taking, eating and drinking bread and wine mediate both an extremely concrete experience of community and a profound and intense certainty. Particularly the Reformed traditions have repeatedly highlighted this certainty:

- Christ has promised "that his body was offered and broken on the cross for me, and his blood shed for me, *as certainly* as I see with my eyes the bread of the Lord broken for me, and the cup communicated to me."
- Christ has promised me that "with his crucified body and shed blood he himself feeds and nourishes my soul to everlasting life, *as certainly* as I receive from the hand of the minister, and taste with my mouth, the bread and cup of the Lord."[1]
- Finally, we read that "by this visible sign and pledge Christ acts *to assure* us that we are really partakers of his true body and blood, through the working of the Holy Ghost, as we receive by the mouth of the body these holy tokens in remembrance of him; and that all his sufferings and obedience are as certainly our own as if we had ourselves suffered and done all in our own persons."[2]

This basic certainty is extremely important. It effects an unsurpassably concrete experience of sacramental presence and an extremely intense experience of community.

In contrast to this intense and very finely tuned experience of commu-

1. Heidelberg Catechism, question 75, in Philip Schaff, *The Creeds of Christendom with a History and Critical Notes,* vol. 3, *The Evangelical Protestant Creeds, with Translations* (New York: Harper and Brothers, 1882), p. 332.

2. Heidelberg Catechism, question 79, p. 335.

nity and action (co-action), the verbal proclamation can be received in many different ways. Its effect is to a large degree dependent upon the skill and talent, the linguistic capability, the sensibility, the intelligence, and many other properties of the persons doing the proclaiming. and of their listeners. The verbal proclamation and its resonance (not merely in the acoustic sense) is also to a large degree dependent upon the time, the circumstances, the concentration, and the experiential and educational backgrounds of the persons among whom the proclamation is taking place. Here and there, with this listener or that one, in each specific situation, there are very different ways in which the verbal proclamation will "hit home" — or not — and will bring about knowledge, illumination, insight, and of course certainty. By contrast, the communal actions of eating and drinking, especially the symbolic actions of eating and drinking, produce an unsurpassable commonality in certainty. With this piece of bread and this drink of wine, I, you, he, she, we, and they take part in this process in the same way. We all see, feel, know that others are participants in the same way. No one can say: I only seemed to be there; I was lost in my thoughts; I didn't get anything out of it. Nor can anyone say: But now I see everything completely differently; We only seemed to understand each other; etc.

At no other place in our life, including that of our spiritual life and our ecclesial community, does it become clear in such a basic way that all human beings are equal before God and that all human beings are bound together before God in the most intense way. In the celebration of holy communion, this is mediated over and over again in unsurpassable, sensuous certainty of human community. This is a great gift that it is impossible to value too highly. It has provided a basis and a root from which has grown a culture of humanity, of law, and of morality — a culture of at least an abstract ethos of equality, which with good reason has been the subject of very intense human labor.[3]

However, this sensuous certainty — *given for us,* here and now given for me as well as for my fellow persons gathered with me, given for them as well as for me — this certainty is not only a powerful bearer of rich blessings; it can also fortify a subjective sense of right on the part of individuals and small groups who isolate themselves and shield themselves against the outside world. Admittedly, we should not universally deni-

3. See Jochen Hörisch, *Brot und Wein: Die Poesie des Abendmahls* (Frankfurt: Suhrkamp, 1992).

grate this attitude, which is hard to avoid in times of persecution. But we must make clear that this attitude falls far short of the full scope of what is happening in holy communion. Concentrating solely on the concretely gathered community and its experiences of certainty can degenerate into group ideology, niche ideology, and deceptive self-certainty. This ideological self-deception is dangerous precisely because all the "neighbors" who are directly present are ready to support and strengthen it. The sensuous and communicative certainty of the Supper, mediated by the symbolic meal, while on the one hand so important and fruitful, is on the other hand always jeopardized when it does not allow itself to be opened, liberated, challenged, and called into question by the phrase "poured out for many."

"Poured out for many": this means that the event of the Supper is not to be related exclusively to those who are concretely celebrating in any particular instance, or to any particular concretely gathered community, although it is concretized in this celebration, in this communion, and in this certainty. In spite of its sensuous mediation, the presence of Christ in the Supper is not exhausted in any particular actual assurance of an intense communion with God and with each other. Instead, the presence of Christ in the Supper, the concrete communion of those who are celebrating, stands in the communion of the countless many, in the communion of the visible and invisible ecumenical church of all times and regions of the world. The celebration of the Supper places participants into this communion, while not dispensing with the certainty, the concrete, sensuous experience and communion. The expression "poured out for many" makes this clear. The "for you" and the "for many" mutually interpret each other, and must do so if we wish to understand what happens in holy communion.

Only if we take seriously the dimensions of the words "poured out for many" will it become clear that the exalted Christ is really present in the Supper — in sensuous, concrete experience — in the entire fullness of his life and in the entire richness of his remembrance (cf. especially chapters 5 and 8). In the celebration of the Supper, in the attendant verbal proclamation, in the symbolic action, in the sensuous mediation, in the symbolic acts of eating and drinking, in the symbolic experience of community — in all these things, the same Christ is present who is also present in all other celebrations of the Supper, in other communities of faith, with precisely this evidence and availability to the senses. Not only does holy communion mediate to those who are participating in any given celebration of the Supper an experience of community and evidence in relation to God and to each other. The Supper also places any given, concretely gathered community into a spatio-temporal fullness of such experiences of evidence. In precisely this way, the Supper binds together the communities of the visible and the invisible church of all times and regions of the world. Not only does it place any given community celebrating the Supper into this context, it also draws the context of the worldwide church of all times and regions of the world into the celebrating community.[4]

Roman Catholic and Orthodox theologies, the latter in a special way, have a great sensitivity to this state of affairs. Again and again, they insist that in the celebration of the Supper we are carrying out the "heavenly liturgy," that in the celebration of the Supper we take part in the "heavenly doxology" and in the "heavenly communion." No matter how little our concrete community may be, the angels are celebrating with us! Can we see in the image of the heavenly hosts gathered around God and God's throne the attempt to think of the representatives of all times and regions of the world, including the representatives of past and future times and regions of the world, gathered in the praise of God?[5] Can we begin to understand the reality, the truth, the material validity contained in this imagistic language? If so, then the notion of the "heavenly liturgy" celebrated in the Supper will not remain foreign to us. Moreover, we will begin to understand why the sacrament can be called "the sacrament of God's reign,"[6] and why it in fact is tied to the joyful eschatological banquet (cf. chapter 7).

Finally, if we begin to take the measure of the broad dimensions expressed by the phrase "for many" — without surrendering the intensity, authenticity, certainty, and all the other qualities of the intimate, solid, concretely gathered community of the meal — we will also understand why the Orthodox and Roman Catholic churches react so sensitively to

4. Cf. "The Unity of the Church" 1979 [OC-O], p. 404: "The one Church on earth exists in the many local Churches whose life is centred on the celebration of the holy Eucharist. . . ."

5. Cf. M. Welker, "Angels and God's Presence in Creation," in *Creation and Reality,* trans. John F. Hoffmeyer (Minneapolis: Fortress, 1999), pp. 54ff.

6. Cf. Alexander Schmemann, *The Eucharist: Sacrament of the Kingdom* (Crestwood, N.Y.: St. Vladimir's Seminary Press, 1988), chap. 2; Horton Davies, *Bread of Life and Cup of Joy: Newer Ecumenical Perspectives on the Eucharist* (Grand Rapids: Eerdmans, 1993), chap. 4, pp. 80ff.

the questions about who presides at the celebration of the meal, and how that celebration is directed. We will understand why they are sensitive about the Supper being celebrated rightly, and why for them it is impossible to be too careful theologically and pastorally in planning the celebration of the Supper and in accompanying the community of the Supper. The Supper that binds together the ecumenical church of all times and regions of the world is not an arena for liturgical experimentation.

The celebration of the Supper creates a basic communion of the ecumenical church not only in this time period, not only in this world — whether the world be defined by media, science, "relevance," or in some other way — but in all times and regions of the world. Therefore we must recognize, understand, preserve, and carefully develop forms that really express this broad communion. If we take the Supper seriously in its spiritual weight and in its ecumenical influence, we will understand the pre-Reformation churches' concern that insufficient oversight in this event that is so central for the church could be devastating. How do we do justice to this concern?

Does the Ministerial Office Guarantee That the Supper Is Celebrated Appropriately? How Can the Churches of the Reformation Respond to the Justified Concerns of the Pre-Reformation Churches?

The celebration of the Supper carries great theological and spiritual weight. Its significance and power of influence overarch epochs and worlds. If we become conscious of these things, we will agree with those who insist that it is impossible to ask for too much competence in those who preside at the Supper and lead its celebration. We will understand those who insist that precisely here an ordained ministry is necessary, that persons with theological formation and spiritual experience must see to it that the sacrament is "administered according to the Gospel."[7] In addition, however — at least

7. "The Augsburg Confession," Article 7, in Theodore G. Tappert, trans. and ed., *The Book of Concord* (Philadelphia: Fortress, 1959), p. 32. Cf. "Ministry and Ordination" 1973 [A-RC], p. 82: "The central act of worship, the eucharist, is the memorial of that reconciliation and nourishes the Church's life for the fulfillment of its mission. Hence it is right that he who has oversight in the Church and is the focus of its unity should preside at the celebration of the eucharist." However, on a biblical basis it is hard to follow the logic of the assertion that "Christ . . . through his minister presides at the Lord's Supper and gives himself sacramentally" (ibid.).

from the Protestant side — we will not want to depend solely upon the ordained bearer of ministerial office. Instead we will consider it important that as far as possible *all* Christians who participate in the celebration of the Supper see to it that, with the help of the bearer of ministerial office, the sacrament is celebrated in accordance with its identity.[8]

At the least, confirmation instruction should strive for and mediate an educational formation in the sacrament which would enable all persons to see to it that the Supper is shaped in the right way. Although participation in the Supper must not be made dependent upon a particular level of development or educational formation (see especially chapter 4), we should still strive for and mediate a general spiritual formation which would make sure that this "summit in the life of the church" is celebrated accordingly. What calls for attention in the context of the "overall pastoral oversight" over the correct celebration of the Supper? Let us take a look back at the insights we have gained:

- Holy communion is to be celebrated as a symbolic communal meal of the gathered community.
- In the celebration of the Supper there should be remembrance of "the

8. See "Dublin Report" 1976 [M-RC], pp. 356ff., and "Amersfoort Statement" 1985 [O-OC], p. 216: "The whole eucharistic community, clergy and people, has an organic part in the performance of the eucharistic celebration." Cf. the contrast between Pentecostal and Roman Catholic positions in "Perspectives on *Koinonia*" 1989 [P-RC], pp. 414-15! Cf. also William Robertson, "The Administration of the Lord's Supper," in Charles R. Gresham and Tom Lawson, *The Lord's Supper: Historical Writings on Its Meaning to the Body of Christ,* pp. 51ff. The difference between Catholics and Reformed in the question of "ministry and sacrament," as described in "The Presence of Christ" 1977 [R-RC], p. 460, is characteristic of the relation between Reformation and pre-Reformation churches: "When it comes to the relation between ministry and sacrament, the Roman Catholics find that the Reformed minimize the extent to which God, in his plan for salvation, has bound himself to the Church, the ministry and the sacraments. The Reformed find that too often Roman Catholic theology minimizes the way the Church, the ministry and the sacraments remain bound to the freedom and the grace of the Holy Spirit." Concerning the relation of the Roman Catholic and Lutheran positions on this question, see the following articles in Paul Empie and T. Austin Murphy, eds., *Eucharist and Ministry: Lutherans and Catholics in Dialogue IV* (Minneapolis: Augsburg, 1979); Harry McSorley, "The Roman Catholic Doctrine of the Competent Minister of the Eucharist in Ecumenical Perspective," pp. 120ff.; John F. Hotchkin, "The Christian Priesthood: Episcopate, Presbyterate and People in the Light of Vatican II," pp. 189ff.; John Reumann, "Ordained Minister and Layman in Lutheranism," pp. 227ff.

night of betrayal," the jeopardizing of the celebrating community both from without and from within.

- This jeopardized community comes together in order to thank God the creator for bread and wine as gifts of creation, and to share these gifts of creation with one another. The community also comes together to meditate upon and to celebrate the transformation of these gifts of creation into gifts of the new creation.
- The gathered community comes together in order to celebrate and to give worthy expression to the unconditional acceptance of human beings by God, and to the unconditional acceptance of human beings among themselves. The enactment of hierarchical relations in the community is out of place in the celebration of the Supper. The celebration of the meal in different "classes" (the clergy behind the sanctuary screen and the community in front of it, or the community in a circle and the "distributors" in front of the altar) contradicts the Supper's intentions. The community of the Supper is not separated into those who give and those who receive, or into those who give and receive, on the one hand, and those who only receive, on the other. The active ministerial office acts in a representative way for the entire community. That office does not represent God or Christ. In order to express both this and the community's overall responsibility for the correct celebration of the Supper, several participants should have a part in distributing the bread and wine, or — still better — all participants should give the bread and wine to their neighbor with the words: The body of Christ, given for you! The blood of Christ, shed for you!
- In all this, the gathered community comes together most of all to celebrate the presence of Christ in the praise of God, in thanksgiving, and in obedient fulfillment of Christ's instructions. With the risen Christ, reconciliation with God and the symbolic reconciliation of human beings with each other are present. Through Christ's presence and through the activity of the Holy Spirit, the meal of the gifts of creation becomes a meal of new creation.
- The gathered community celebrates the presence of the risen Christ. In the risen Christ the remembered historical Jesus, the proclaimed crucified Christ, and the coming Human One are present. Jesus Christ is present in the fullness of his person and at the same time in the greatest sensuous certainty, which is mediated by the giving and taking, the eating and drinking of bread and wine.
- Christ's coming to presence in the holy communion means that not

only do the night of betrayal and the self-jeopardizing of the celebrating community become present, but so does the complete lostness of the whole world under the power of sin, which becomes manifest in Christ's cross. The Supper makes present the need and misery of the world, which with religion, law, politics, and morality stands against God's presence.

- But the Supper also makes present God's faithfulness and love, through which God delivers human beings from this misery and need, liberates them from the power of sin, and makes them witnesses of God's presence and bearers of the divine life.
- In the Supper the faithful are taken into this presence of the risen and coming Christ. They are led on the way in which God raises up creatures and sets them apart for participation in the divine glory.
- In the Supper the faithful are placed into the broad memory of Christ, inasmuch as they acquire a share in the fullness of the presence of Jesus Christ, and give others a share in that fullness.
- In the Supper the faithful are taken into the ecumenical church of all times and regions of the world. They are symbolically both liberated from the power of sin, and set apart and sanctified for communion with God.
- In the Supper — and here we are looking ahead to the subsequent chapters — the faithful are taken into the divine peace, and made familiar with the presence and activity of the triune God.

It is not the task of only the ordained ministry and the leaders celebrating the Supper to see to it that all this is not obscured, that it comes at least incipiently to expression in the proclamation and the liturgy. In principle, it is the task of every Christian to remain attentive to all this and to draw attention to it.[9] In confirmation instruction (or in analogous forms of ecclesial educational formation) at the least, every Christian should be introduced into this mature responsibility, right, and competence.

9. See *Niagara Report* 1987 [A-L], p. 36: "We believe that a ministry of pastoral oversight *(episcope),* exercised in personal, collegial and communal ways, is necessary to witness to and safeguard the unity and apostolicity of the Church."

Should Children Also Be Admitted to the Supper?

Participation in the Supper cannot and must not be refused to any baptized person. Neither an absence of bodily or mental health, nor deficient education, development, or morality can be a reason for excluding persons from the celebration of holy communion. Churches and church communities should, however, strive for the greatest possible maturity and competence of those participating in the celebration of the meal. This maturity and competence in the theology of the Supper should be mediated by confirmation (or at a similar level of the educational formation of those who are growing up). The greatest possible number of persons participating in the Supper should know what the celebration of the Supper is about and how the Supper is celebrated in accordance with its identity. The baptized and confirmed members of the community should accompany and support the ordained ministers in their overall oversight *(episcope)* over the correct celebration of the Supper.

This basic orientation enables us to take a clear position on the question of whether baptized children should be admitted to the Supper. In many Christian communities this question is still among those problems riddled with discord and uncertainty.[10] Those who argue against infant baptism see here an opportunity to strengthen their position: It is illogical to baptize infants and then to postpone their participation in the Supper until confirmation. Therefore we should admit only mature Christians to the sacramental events of the worship service.

Those who see that the point in time in which maturity is attained cannot be defined in a clear and universally binding way will choose a more differentiated approach. On the one hand, we must start from the assumption that participation in the Supper must not be refused to any baptized person. Thus we will also welcome baptized children at the cele-

10. Cf. Martin Lienhard, ed., *Mit Kindern Abendmahl feiern: Modelle, Reflexionen, Materialien* (Munich: Kaiser, 1978); Eberhard Kenntner, *Abendmahl mit Kindern: Versuch einer Grundlegung unter Berücksichtigung der geschichtlichen Wurzeln der gegenwärtigen Diskussion in Deutschland,* 3rd ed. (Gütersloh: Gütersloher Verlagshaus, 1989); Geiko Müller-Fahrenholz, ed., . . . *and do not hinder them: An ecumenical plea for the admission of children to the eucharist,* Faith and Order Paper 109 (Geneva: WCC, 1981). Cf. also the position taken by the Evangelical Church in Baden, Germany, in Max Thurian, ed., *Churches Respond to BEM: Official Responses to the "Baptism, Eucharist and Ministry" Text,* vol. 5, Faith and Order Paper 143 (Geneva: World Council of Churches, 1987), pp. 44-45.

bration of the meal, if this is what they, their parents, and their congregations wish. On the other hand, we will attach a lot of weight to striving for the greatest possible maturity and competence in the theology of the Supper on the part of those who participate in the celebration of the meal. The advice to children, parents, and congregations will be to encourage children's participation in the Supper if it serves the cause of growth in maturity and competence in the theology of the Supper. Since this is a matter of judgment, and since different styles of piety and different conceptions of education formation will shape the decisions, we should no more expect a unilinear development in this matter than in the question of how often we should celebrate the Supper. Some persons will be of the opinion that children cannot celebrate the Supper often enough, while others will see in that position a failure to attend to the aspect of maturity. Some parents and congregations will suggest to their children that they start joining in the celebration of the Supper only after confirmation, while others will see in that position an intimidating legalism. An American theology student told me how an experience in a celebration of holy communion had weighed upon her for years: as a small child the bread had been put into her hand — and then taken away. In my own case, the question of my five-year-old daughter would not let me go: Do you let the little children go hungry at the Supper?

The advice not to let children's participation in the Supper become a routine matter, but to pay attention to whether they are thereby maturing in their theology of the Supper, makes possible an ordered flexibility that gives a shared orientation to various styles of piety. All positions should be bound together by the insight that children should not be deprived of explanations of what happens in holy communion. As many as possible of those who participate in the Supper should know what happens in holy communion and should see to it that the Supper is properly celebrated. Precisely here the "priesthood of all believers" can acquire a credible form. Precisely here the mature community can help the ordained minister so that a central event of ecclesial life does not serve the self-presentation of the office of ordained ministry, but rather is shaped in accord with the instructions of Jesus Christ.[11]

11. Cf. *Toward Church Fellowship* 1990 [L-R], p. 24.

Results

The phrases "given for you" and "poured out for many" address the concrete, gathered community and the ecumenical church of all times and regions of the world. The celebration of the Supper places a given gathered community into the ecumenical context and draws the worldwide church into the celebrating community. The great theological and spiritual importance of the celebration of the meal, and its influence and formative power throughout the ecumenical church, enable us to recognize that holy communion is not an arena for liturgical experimentation. We must be responsible in shaping it and cautious in reshaping it.

It becomes understandable why churches have insisted — with particular emphasis on the part of the pre-Reformation churches — that the ordained ministry must see to it that the sacrament is "administered according to the Gospel." However, without downplaying the significance of the ordained minister in presiding at and directing the Supper, an evangelical understanding of the Supper will place value on the gathered community's maturity in the theology of the Supper. To the extent possible, all Christians who participate in the celebration of the Supper should contribute to the goal of the sacrament being celebrated in accordance with its identity. In any case the enactment of hierarchical relations in the community is out of place in the celebration of the Supper. The celebration of the Supper in different "classes" does not correspond to the way in which it was instituted.

It is one of the tasks of spiritual formation to put as many people in Christian churches as possible in a position to accompany the ordained minister with attention and alertness in shaping the celebration of the Supper, or to themselves contribute to that shaping. This insight also provides orientation concerning the question of whether children should be admitted to holy communion. The Supper cannot be and must not be refused to any baptized person. But children's participation in the Supper should serve their growth in maturity and competence in the theology of the Supper.

CHAPTER 10

Liberation from the Power of Sin — or Preservation for Eternal Life?

An Ecumenical Controversy That Still Impairs the Shared Celebration of the Supper at the Dawn of the Third Millennium

What happens in holy communion? The tenth answer is: *In the celebration of holy communion, human beings are liberated from the power of sin. In this liberation they are given a share in God's eternal life. They are not merely restored as members of the "good creation," but are raised up as members of the "new creation."*

Forgiveness of Sins — Pledge of Eternal Life

What happens in holy communion: liberation from the power of sin or preservation for eternal life? It is tempting to say "both/and!" It is tempting to assert that the synoptic gospels give more emphasis to the aspect of the acceptance of sinners and the forgiveness of sin, while the Johannine texts highlight more the preservation for eternal life. The two are not mutually exclusive. "Baptism, Eucharist and Ministry" offers this Solomonic formulation in part 2, under the heading "The Meaning of the Eucharist": "In accordance with Christ's promise, each baptized member of the body of Christ receives in the eucharist the assurance of the forgiveness of sins (Matt. 26:28) and the pledge of eternal life (John 6:51-58)."[1]

In connection with the "words of institution," Matthew 26:27-28 explicitly provides the synoptic perspective: "Then he took a cup, and after giving thanks he gave it to them, saying, 'Drink from it, all of you; for this is my blood of the covenant, which is poured out for many for the forgiveness of sins.'"

The Johannine perspective is formulated in a text (Jn 6:51c-58) that many scholars take to be a "deutero-Johannine addition."[2]

> The bread that I will give is my flesh, (I give it) for the life of the world. . . .
>
> 54 Those who eat my flesh and drink my blood have eternal life, and I will raise them up on the last day;
> 55 for my flesh is truly food and my blood is truly drink.
> 56 Those who eat my flesh and drink my blood abide in me, and I in them.
> 57 Just as the living Father sent me, and I live because of the Father, so whoever eats my flesh will live because of me.
> 58 This is the bread that came down from heaven, not like that which your ancestors ate, and they died. But the one who eats this bread will live forever.

However, the Solomonic assertion that we are merely dealing with two different perspectives masks an important difference between the two aspects (liberation from sin — preservation for eternal life).[3] It masks subtle but wide-reaching differences in the larger churches' understanding of the Supper. These differences bring with them conflict-laden attitudes toward the questions: Is it permissible for us to offer table fellowship to each other? Can we celebrate the Supper in common?

1. "Baptism, Eucharist and Ministry" 1982 [WCC], p. 476.

2. See Ferdinand Hahn, "Abendmahl I: Neues Testament," *Die Religion in Geschichte und Gegenwart,* vol. 1, 4th ed. (Tübingen, 1998), pp. 10-13.

3. "Ways to Community" 1980 [L-RC], p. 229, emphasizes that "it is necessary to rethink the understanding of sin," but does not even sketch the task. Cf. Leo Hay, *Eucharist: A Thanksgiving Celebration,* Message of the Sacraments 3-A (Wilmington, Del.: Glazier, 1989), pp. 84ff.

Painful Ecumenical Differences Despite Great Commonality

On the surface, all the larger churches recognize in their documents of consensus that holy communion is about the forgiveness of sins. But if we study the documents more closely, we quickly encounter notable differences:

- For Lutherans, the Supper is above all about the forgiveness of sin, understood as a reversal of human existence that is beyond our control.
- The Reformed underscore and develop this element of being beyond our control, inasmuch as they emphasize that the forgiveness of sin is not borne in an unmediated way by the word of the Supper, but rather occurs through the activity of the Holy Spirit. They also insist that the forgiveness of sin is central to the Supper.
- Compared to the two Reformation convictions named above, the Roman Catholic position lies closer to the Lutheran position, since the sacrifice of the mass, by the mere fact of its being carried out *(ex opere operato),* provides forgiveness of sin.
- The Orthodox position can be formulated in the following way: although forgiveness of sins by means of the Supper is not excluded, the connection between Christ, the Spirit, and the church is so close that there can be no talk of a radical reversal of human existence. In the sacrament the faithful receive spiritual nourishment on their way through the world; they are strengthened on their way to participation in the divine glory, indeed, on their way to divinization.[4]

Although one can still speak of the forgiveness of sin, we have hereby arrived at the position of "preservation for eternal life." Here the moment that is so important to the Lutheran position in particular and the Reformation position in general, the moment of discontinuity, of the reversal of human existence in the forgiveness of sin, becomes unclear. The proclamation of Christ's death, the remembrance of the cross, the recognition of one's own unworthiness, the recognition of Christ's betrayal as a threat to be overcome — here all these things sharply recede or completely fade away.

In his evaluation of the ecumenical conversations, Eckhard Lessing has rightly emphasized that although all churches name the forgiveness of

4. See Alexander Schmemann, *For the Life of the World* (Crestwood, N.Y.: St. Vladimir's Seminary Press, 1995), pp. 23ff.

sin as a fruit of the eucharist, only the Reformation churches regard it as central.[5] According to Lessing, in "Baptism, Eucharist and Ministry" as well the connection between sin and the forgiveness of sin "receives only insufficient consideration."[6] There are at least two reasons why the churches of the Reformation have not known how to bring the theme of the forgiveness of sin into the ecumenical conversations in such a way that this theme would remain central to the theological substance of those conversations.

- They have not worked with sufficient insistence to counteract the systematic elision of the "night of betrayal," and they have not prevented the "proclamation of the Lord's death" from receiving only insufficient weight and development (cf. chapters 2 and 6).
- They have depended too much on trying to grasp and articulate in a materially appropriate way the existence of the sinner before God. "Baptism, Eucharist and Ministry" strikingly demonstrates both that and how the theological concern of the Reformation churches is lost in the process.

"Baptism, Eucharist and Ministry" starts out by insisting that in the Supper God is first and foremost the giver. Christ gives. The impartation of the gift and the dependence of the recipients are primary; the act of taking part and the configuration of that act are secondary. But this beginning and the attendant talk of the forgiveness of sin do not persist through the document. Indeed they increasingly fade away. For a sensitive interpretation, this displacement already becomes clear in paragraph 3 (II A), when the text says that the eucharist is "the great thanksgiving to the Father . . . for everything accomplished by God now in the Church and in the world in spite of the sins of human beings."[7] The words "in spite of" can only mean that the Supper is no longer to be regarded as the action of God or Christ centrally engaging and struggling with sin in church and world, but rather as an action

5. Cf., though, initial steps for example in "Chambésy Statement" 1983 [O-OC], p. 202; as well as in "Dialogue on Mission" 1984 [E-RC], p. 463. See also the difference between Lutherans and Baptists in *A Message to Our Churches* 1990 [B-L], pp. 35-36.

6. Eckhard Lessing, *Abendmahl,* Bensheimer Ökumenische Studienhefte 1 (Göttingen: Vandenhoeck, 1993), p. 131; cf. pp. 126ff.

7. "Baptism, Eucharist and Ministry" 1982 [WCC], p. 476.

that also "passes sin by," so to speak. It is then not surprising that the aspect of the Supper as pledge of eternal life substantively suppresses the aspect of the forgiveness of sin. This becomes clear in two ways. On the one hand, the church is presented with increasing emphasis as the anticipation of God's reign. On the other hand, the forgiveness of sin is thematized in paragraph 21 among liturgy, greeting of peace, and intercession only as "the mutual forgiveness of sins."[8] Lessing has put this problem clearly: "The communion in Christ's love could indeed be understood to mean primarily the church's being called out of the world of sin and death. To be sure, [the Lima Report] does not deny this idea. But the weight lies on the church as anticipatory representation of the reign of God."[9]

According to our investigation of what happens in holy communion, if Lima represents a theology of the Supper capable of generating ecumenical consensus, then such a theology shows not just happy commonalities, but very significant differences. If the theme of the forgiveness of sin receives "insufficient consideration," this means that none of the following are taken seriously enough:

- the entanglement of the entire church under the power of sin;
- the night of betrayal as the context in which the Supper is instituted;
- the memory of the cross, the proclamation of Christ's death;
- the fact that the recognition of the resurrection remains under attack;
- the relativity of the "for us" in relation to the "for many": that is, concretely, the distance between the gathered community and the one, holy, apostolic church, not to mention the heavenly eucharist, however much the gathered community indeed belongs to both;
- the fact that we are still awaiting Christ's *parousia.*

Unfortunately Lima was and is anything but a "misstep." "Baptism, Eucharist and Ministry" is the consequence of a long process of coming to an understanding, into which the churches of the Reformation were unable to bring their position with the theological clarity and persuasiveness that would have been necessary to guide ecumenical theological understanding in the right direction. "Baptism, Eucharist and Ministry" is above all the fruit of ecumenical understanding in a global context in

8. "Baptism, Eucharist and Ministry" 1982 [WCC], p. 479.

9. Lessing, *Abendmahl,* pp. 126-27.

which the word "sin" has become an incomprehensible or even laughable expression (cf. chapter 6).[10]

The Church of Sinners Graced by God? Why Can't the Churches of the Reformation Make a Better Case for Their Theological Concern?

Let us consider only the conversations concerning holy communion within Germany, within Europe, and among the churches of the Reformation, from Halle by way of Arnoldshain to the Leuenberg Agreement. It is striking that, although the significance of the forgiveness of sin in the context of the Supper is regularly emphasized, the conversations are ruled by a striking uncertainty concerning the place of that forgiveness.

Arnoldshain says in thesis 2.2 that the Supper, "like the sermon, baptism, and the particular assurance of the forgiveness of sins, belongs to the ways in which Christ appropriates to us the gifts of the saving gospel." This raises the embarrassing question of how then the forgiveness of sins in the Supper and the "particular assurance of the forgiveness of sins" are different from each other, and how they are tied together. Is the "particular assurance of the forgiveness of sins" a consequence of the devastating individualization and privatization of the concept of sin?[11] Do we have here, instead of the power of sin against which the celebration of the Supper is directed, only "my particular sin," to which the "particular assurance of the forgiveness of sins" reacts?

The fourth Arnoldshain thesis is similarly unclear:

> Our Lord gave his body into death for all and poured out his blood for all. Through his word of promise, the crucified and risen Lord lets himself be taken by us in that body and blood with bread and wine.

10. Cf. Sigrid Brandt et al., *Sünde: Ein unverständlich gewordenes Thema* (Neukirchen-Vluyn: Neukirchener, 1997); Elisabeth Moltmann-Wendel, "Ich, ich und meine Sünden," in *Wir Frauen und das Herrenmahl* (Stuttgart, 1996), pp. 13ff. Martin Marty's little book *The Lord's Supper* (Philadelphia: Fortress, 1980) shows that even in a secularized society the Supper can be understood and highly esteemed as an event of the forgiveness of sin.

11. Cf. A. Peters, "Bupe, Beichte, Schuldvergebung," in Peters, *Rechenschaft des Glaubens: Aufsätze*, ed. R. Slenczka (Göttingen: Vandenhoeck, 1984); Peters, "Christliche Seelsorge im Horizont der drei Glaubensartikel: Aspekte einer theologischen Anthropologie," *Theologische Literaturzeitung* 114 (1989): 641ff.

> By the power of the Holy Spirit, he thereby takes us into the victory of his dominion, so that by faith in his promise we have forgiveness of sins, life, and blessedness.

Thesis 6.3 adds that in the Supper "the Lord establishes the beginning of a new humanity in the midst of sinners to whom grace has been shown." If we take these statements together, it becomes very difficult to give a thoughtful account of the process of *liberation* from sin. The positions of the Reformation churches, too, move toward the perspective which highlights the Supper as "pledge of eternal life."

The reason for this can be precisely defined. The moralization of the biblical concept of sin in the modern period made that concept incomprehensible. In an — unsuccessful — attempt to articulate the relation between God and sinful human beings, theology (especially *dialectical theology*) emphasized God's absolute power over human beings and their powerlessness before God. It is not we who act in the Supper, but God alone, Christ alone. We are sinners — therefore it must be God alone and only God who acts upon us. Leuenberg puts it this way: "In the Lord's Supper the risen Christ imparts himself in his body and blood, given up for all, through his word of promise with bread and wine. He thereby grants us forgiveness of sins, and sets us free for a new life of faith. He enables us to experience anew that we are members of his body."[12]

As the context shows, the accent is supposed to lie on Christ's "self-impartation," Christ's "self-giving." Christ is giver and gift! However, this emphasis on God's sovereignty in this process — an emphasis typical of dialectical theology — only apparently gives appropriate expression to our being as sinners, our jeopardization, our self-destruction, our misery and need. The problem is that the theology of mere sovereignty and power can be effortlessly channeled into the "pledge of eternal life" idea. "He enables us to experience anew that we are members of his body." To be sure, this line of thought is by no means false or theologically erroneous. But it cannot give adequate expression to the actual concern of the Reformation churches, especially of Lutheranism: The Supper is about the danger of sin and the drama of the forgiveness of sin. In the perhaps unimpressive, but tremendously rich interconnection of doxology, remembrance of Christ, invocation of the Spirit, breaking, sharing, distributing, eating, and drinking of bread and wine, and unconditional mutual

12. *Leuenberg Agreement*, p. 148.

acceptance — at the heart of all this is an act of deliverance, an act in which human beings are rescued from lostness under the power of sin.

The Reformation churches' inability to bring across their theological concern also becomes clear in conversations on the global level with Roman Catholics and Orthodox. In the important Lutheran–Roman Catholic text "The Eucharist" (1978) we find in paragraph 10 on the one hand the laudable formulation that in the celebration of the Supper "the reality of sin becomes apparent and demands recollection and confession."[13] But on the other hand this "becoming apparent" stands in a large collection of many other things which also become apparent in the Supper. We also encounter in this text the already quoted formulation which will later make its way into "Baptism, Eucharist and Ministry": the eucharist is "the great thanksgiving to the Father for everything . . . which He accomplishes now in the Church and in the world *in spite of* the sins of men."[14]

The Condemnations of the Reformation Era: Do They Still Divide?, edited by Karl Lehmann and Wolfhart Pannenberg, shows still more strongly a blindness in its theology of sin. When that volume asserts that "the dispute about the forgiveness of sins as fruit of the Eucharist may also count as having been clarified and theologically settled," we must simply regard that claim as concealing the actual state of affairs.[15] To be sure, the text thematizes the controverted question of "whether in the eucharist Christ is present primarily to the community united with God, or to the believing human being, who as a believer is also a sinner." But the problem of the difference between impartation and participation, the problem of the forgiveness of sin as a question of our enduring dependence on God's word addressed to us and for us — this problem is not clearly recognized, or in any case not thematized.[16]

What is actually happening is that the "forgiveness of sins perspective" is being shifted into the "pledge of eternal life perspective." The Lehmann/Pannenberg text considers "whether it would not be less misleading to give another name [than "forgiveness of sins"] to just this all-embracing aspect of the divine salvation," calling it instead "the dawn of

13. "The Eucharist" 1978 [L-RC], p. 194.

14. "The Eucharist" 1978 [L-RC], p. 199.

15. Karl Lehmann and Wolfhart Pannenberg, eds., *The Condemnations of the Reformation Era: Do They Still Divide?*, trans. Margaret Kohl (Minneapolis: Fortress, 1990), p. 116. Lessing, *Abendmahl*, p. 85, politely characterizes this assertion as "bold."

16. Cf. Lessing, *Abendmahl*, pp. 86ff.

the rule of God (Mark 1:15, and frequently), the love of God (Romans 5), koinonia (1 Cor. 10:16f.)."[17] We find this tendency clearly marked in the so-called Helsinki Report (1983) of the conversations between Lutherans and Orthodox. There we read in paragraph 28: "While both our Churches have traditionally understood the effects of the eucharist in terms of forgiveness, Anglicans and Lutherans today also wish to stress its fruits in the building up of the community of the Church" etc. The tendency becomes clear in the next sentence: "In the eucharist we already have a foretaste of the eternal joy of God's kingdom."[18] As correct as this is, it is equally true that the perspective of the forgiveness of sin must not be lost in ideas of "pledge" and "foretaste."[19] There is a real need for consistent theological countermeasures against this trend![20]

On the basis of a decidedly biblical-theology approach, the Reformed–Roman Catholic consensus document "The Presence of Christ in Church and World" (1977) regards sin and death as powers enslaving human beings. The text repeatedly emphasizes that in the Supper the power of Christ, revealed in cross and resurrection, contends against these powers. Lessing concedes that of all Protestant-Catholic consensus documents, this one best preserves the difference between Christ and the church and most clearly retains the theme of the forgiveness of sin. Lessing further recognizes that the extent to which Catholics here engage Protestant positions is simply astounding.

Consequences for Sharing the Eucharistic Meal

What is supposedly a mere subtlety in the theological weighting of the balance between forgiveness of sins and preservation for eternal life has major

17. Lehmann and Pannenberg, eds., *The Condemnations of the Reformation Era,* p. 111.

18. *Anglican-Lutheran Dialogue: The Report of the European Commission* (London: SPCK, 1983), p. 12.

19. A laudable exception is the so-called Meissen Statement, *On the Way to Visible Unity.* In this statement of agreement between the Anglican church and the German Evangelical church we find at least the beginnings of a critique of a false understanding of sin and forgiveness of sin. And the text explicitly cites 1 Cor 11:26: "For as often as you eat this bread and drink the cup, you proclaim the Lord's death until he comes."

20. The phrase that the church "always includes sinners" contains a typical trivialization of the power of sin. That formulation makes it sound as if the problem was merely individual cases. Cf. "Facing Unity" 1984 [L-RC], p. 34.

consequences for the decision whether ecumenical communion in the Supper is accorded or refused to Christians of other churches. The Reformation churches insist that we are all human beings who live from God's sin-forgiving and liberating grace. We receive a share in this grace of God in the celebration of the Supper. Therefore we cannot refuse communion in this meal to other baptized Christians. Whoever refuses communion in the Supper to baptized Christians should instead seriously examine whether he or she is celebrating the Supper "worthily" (see chapter 4).

The churches that place "preservation for eternal life" in the foreground evidently cannot identify with the Reformation position at the dawn of the third millennium. They want to spare their members the threat that supposedly lies in a shared meal which in their view would not be celebrated in the right shared faith.[21] Will help come from a clearer mediation of the Reformation position than we have found in the ecumenical documents? That remains to be seen in the discussion of the next years or decades. We have tried to make clear that joint work on the theme of "sin and forgiveness of sin" or "liberation from the power of sin" will open up new dimensions in the understanding of the Supper, of faith, and of the church of Christ (cf. especially chapters 2 and 6).

Ecumenical labor on this theme will benefit not only the churches and the growth of their communion, but also their shared influence on the modern world. It will benefit the influence of the Christian churches on a world that has withdrawn and alienated itself from religion by means of a relatively clueless process of moralization. If the churches of the Reformation are able to provide better access to a truth that has previously been obscured (by themselves as well), ecumenical communion in the Supper will become a fruit of the shared knowledge of truth. Interest in hierarchical self-preservation and the fear of such interest, which continually emerge as hindrances on the way to full ecumenical communion, are not good sources of counsel. The claim that only the full mutual recognition of ministerial offices allows eucharistic communion has stirred up this fear. By contrast, the "Malta Report" insists: "Unclarity concerning a common doctrine of the ministerial office still makes for difficulties in reciprocal intercommunion agreements. However, the realization of

21. See the clear rejection of "intercommunion" in "Dublin Statement" 1984 [A-O], pp. 14-15. Cf. G. C. Berkouwer, *The Sacraments,* Studies in Dogmatics, reprint (Grand Rapids: Eerdmans, 1981), pp. 279ff.

eucharistic fellowship should not depend exclusively on full recognition of the offices of the ministry."[22]

With irresistible power, the knowledge of truth will free the way to ecumenical communion. If in the Supper all human beings are continually liberated anew from the power of sin, from closure against God, and from closure against each other — if this is true, then no power of this world can or will be able to block all churches of Christ from growing together into full eucharistic, anamnetic, and sacramental communion.

Results

In the celebration of the Supper, are human beings liberated from the power of sin (Mt 26:27-28) or preserved for eternal life (Jn 6:51ff.)? In their ecumenical conversations, the larger churches on the one hand insist that both perspectives must be bound together. On the other hand, they establish a differing balance between the two, behind which lurks a deep ecumenical difference.

The churches of the Reformation emphasize that the forgiveness of sin brings with it a liberating reversal of human existence. The pre-Reformation churches emphasize that the Supper preserves the church on its way to eternal life. Since the Reformation position regards the church as a church of sinners who need continually to be set free by God, it places great value on the communion of all baptized Christians in the Supper. By contrast, out of an interest in the preservation of the church for eternal life, the pre-Reformation churches object to an ecumenical meal community.

The Reformation churches must try harder to give the pre-Reformation churches a biblically grounded familiarity with the Reformation churches' understanding of sin and forgiveness of sin (cf. chapters

22. "Malta Report" 1972 [L-RC], p. 186. A circumspect observation of the difficulties on the way to sacramental fellowship is provided by Markus Eham, *Gemeinschaft im Sakrament? Die Frage nach der Möglichkeit sakramentaler Gemeinschaft zwischen katholischen und nichtkatholischen Christen: Zur ekklesiologischen Dimension der ökumenischen Frage,* 2 vols., Europäische Hochschulschriften 293 (Frankfurt: Peter Lang, 1986). An exemplary instance of a successful process of coming to an understanding, prepared with theological carefulness, is recorded in the volume edited by William A. Norgren and William G. Rusch: *"Toward Full Communion" and "Concordat of Agreement": Lutheran-Episcopal Dialogue, Series III* (Minneapolis: Augsburg, 1991).

2 and 6). Not only would the Reformation churches be providing an invaluable service to ecumenical understanding, and not only would they be working toward the realization of the ecumenical meal community. They would also be serving a culture which an almost blind trust in morality has caused to lose touch with an understanding of sin and its power.

CHAPTER 11

"God's Peace Be with You! "— "Go in Peace!"

The Supper as Celebration of Preservation, Liberation, and Renewal

The eleventh answer to the question "What happens in holy communion?" is: *The celebration of holy communion establishes a creative peace. The thanksgiving to God (eucharist), the remembrance of Christ (anamnesis), and the invocation of the Holy Spirit (epiklesis) bring to expression the various dimensions of this peace.*

Making Peace and Greeting with Peace Before, After, or In the Celebration of the Supper?

When I heard for the first time that an intrahuman act of reconciliation, an act of "making peace," could or ought to take place *before* the celebration of the Supper, I had no idea what to make of it. My brother and I had just been confirmed, and were now allowed to go to communion. In the morning before the worship service our Catholic grandmother, who was visiting, asked us if we had "reconciled" with each other and with our parents. Since we had not had a fight, and since we also had not had any dispute with our parents, I was disturbed and asked my mother for advice. With a reply of "Nonsense!" I was left in perplexity.

Later I heard that this was supposedly a "a Catholic custom," but that also in rural Protestant congregations disputes between persons or families were sometimes ritually brought to an end before the celebration of the Supper: The pastor made the sign of the cross over the reconciling handshake of the disputants. I learned that in the background stood Jesus' instruction: "So when you are offering your gift at the altar, if you remember that your brother or sister has something against you, leave your gift there before the altar and go; first be reconciled to your brother or sister, and then come and offer your gift" (Mt 5:23-24).[1]

If the peace accord before the meal remained foreign to me for a long time, the greeting of peace *after* the meal soon became a ritual routine to which I did not give a second thought. Presumably it would have bothered me even as a youth if after the Supper the pastor would have concluded not with "Go in peace!" but with "See you later!" or "Have a good day!" But beyond a vague ritual sensibility the greeting of peace did not occupy my attention. Other ritual phrases were also able to serve as the "dismissal" after the meal.

I started — hesitantly — to reflect upon the greeting of peace when it appeared in the course of the service of holy communion. In the 1960s I heard of ecumenical celebrations of the supper in California in which such cordial "peace greetings" were exchanged that an American colleague enthusiastically exclaimed: "Oh, I love kissing all these little nuns!" (Today, of course, this does not seem so funny to us, because we hear more clearly the male-chauvinist overtone.) Ten years later I experienced these embraces (somewhat stiffer on the east coast, somewhat more demonstrative on the west coast) in celebrations of the Supper, and somehow they "fit" in the cordial atmosphere of the North American congregations that I had the privilege of getting to know. More awkward were the embarrassed handshakes that in the subsequent years in many German Sunday services followed the charge: "Recognize one another as sisters and brothers . . ."

In typically European Protestant situations, I found the most convincing greeting of peace to be the one passed through the rows with the words "God's peace be with you" and the response "And also with you." The charge: "May God's peace go throughout the world!" was thus followed by a symbolic action that gave expression to the passing on of peace in and through the gathered community. In the circle of those gathered

1. In its response to "Baptism, Eucharist and Ministry," the Roman Catholic Church interpreted the self-examination spoken of in 1 Cor 11:28 as "need for previous reconciliation of sinners" (Max Thurian, ed., *Churches Respond to BEM: Official Responses to the "Baptism, Eucharist and Ministry" Text,* vol. 6, Faith and Order Paper 144 [Geneva: World Council of Churches, 1988], p. 18).

around the altar this greeting of peace (often passed on with both hands), either before or after the distribution of the elements, also had a persuasive effect on me. But what is the meaning of the greeting of peace in the various phases of holy communion?

The Multidimensionality of Peace

Is the act of making peace the presupposition of participation in holy communion, or does the celebration of the Supper establish peace? If we recognize what happens in holy communion, we can clear away this false alternative. The celebration of the Supper moves by a process of potentiation: We start by gratefully joining our voices in the peace of creation; then against the background of the night of betrayal and the proclamation of cross and death *(Agnus Dei)* we ask for Christ's saving peace; the process culminates as we invoke the Holy Spirit, the liberating and renewing power of peace, a power which lifts creatures up to become bearers of God's presence on earth.

"God's Peace Be with You!" — "And Also with You!" Joining in the Peace of Creation

In some German churches at the beginning of the Supper we have the liturgical charge (following Col 3:13): "The peace of God be with you all. Let no one be against another, let no one be a hypocrite. Forgive as you have been forgiven; welcome one another as Christ has welcomed you to the glory of God." What does this mean? It does not mean that this expression of peace between human beings is already the sum total of the process of reconciliation celebrated in the Supper (see chapter 3). With the greeting of peace in the framework of thanksgiving to the Creator *(eucharistia),* the faithful join their voices in the peace of creation, which appears with bread and wine, gifts of creation. The fact that bread and wine as gifts of creation are given to us is already cause to thank the Creator and to rejoice in the creative activity of the Holy Spirit. As gifts of creation, bread and wine are inconceivable without a successful interplay of nature and culture, of human and non-human creaturehood. Creative, far-reaching, interconnected processes must succeed in order for bread and wine to be available for the celebration of the Supper. The grateful joining of voices in the greeting of peace belongs to thanksgiving for rich blessings that flow from the activity of God and the divine Spirit — an activity made tangible in the gifts of creation. Just as the presence of the gifts of creation is not automatic, so is it not automatic that human beings are able to gather in health, joy, and openness to worship. With the greeting of peace, participants in the Supper underscore their thanksgiving and their readiness jointly to enter into the process of liberation and renewal by God's presence and activity.

"Christ, Lamb of God, Give Us Your Peace"

The renewal by God's presence and activity in holy communion is not some harmless happening. It is a dramatic event. The "remembrance" of Christ, the *anamnesis,* brings into view the night of betrayal and the death of Christ. The fragility and the brokenness of the peace of creation become manifest. Before the cross of Christ, it is possible to recognize the power of sin, which plunges human beings into lovelessness, hopelessness, enmity toward each other, and an absence of peace between each other.

This situation of the greatest misery and need is encompassed by the "peace of Christ," in which human beings recognize the great danger in which they stand and by which they are continually threatened. The peace of Christ imparts to them the powers of liberation and of new creation. In the celebration of the Supper, bread and wine as gifts of creation become gifts of the new creation. In them Christ himself and his indestructible peace are present in the midst of the fragile peace of creation. Bread and wine serve not only the actual and symbolic strengthening of creatures and their community. They also build up the "body of Christ": that is, they build up the bearers of Christ's presence on earth. The reign of God proclaimed by Jesus Christ, which with its powers of forgiveness and of love is unqualifiedly superior to the powers of this world, is now "in advent," along with Jesus Christ's entry into dominion. A new reality, the presence of God, permeates the reality of creation. God's presence liberates creation, renews it, lifts it up, exalts it. God is experienced not only as creator and preserver of this world; in Christ God is experienced as savior, who rescues this world from its self-jeopardization, lostness, and helplessness against the power of sin. God's good, creative Spirit is experienced as the Spirit of liberation and new creation given by Christ. In the invocation of the Spirit *(epiklesis),* the human beings participating in the celebration of the Supper ask for the Holy Spirit to come and work mightily among them.

"The God of Peace Sanctify You Through and Through . . ." — "Go in Peace!"

The persons who have participated in the celebration of the Supper are blessed and sent forth with a greeting of peace. This greeting of peace points them not only toward the (restored) peace of creation. They are now surrounded by the peace of Christ; they are filled with the peace of the Holy Spirit. In the power of the Holy Spirit, God draws near to human beings, lays hold of them, and makes them bearers of the divine presence. Human beings receive a share in the powers of the "new creation." God deems them worthy of an existence that in faith, love, and hope resists the power of sin and of death. They receive a share in "eternal life," in divine life. God deems them worthy to bear witness to this life and to incorporate it. One cannot think or speak too highly of life in this peace. The biblical texts say that people are "sanctified," that they are "lifted up," that they are renewed in the "image of God," that they become "members of the body of Christ," that in Christ they become a "new creation," that God's Spirit transforms them "from glory to glory."

A great joy, a high and festive mood corresponds to this assurance of peace. The greeting of peace at the beginning of the meal prepares people's hearts for the celebration of the Supper. They then ask for Christ's peace in view of the jeopardization of communion between human beings and God and among each other, in view of the world's sin and lostness as revealed by Christ's cross. Against this background, the reception of the gift of peace mediated by God's Spirit gives every reason for great, indeed boundless joy. For this reason the Supper can be concluded only in a festive and joyful mood.

In his *Liturgics,* Rainer Volp has rightly called attention to the fact that the correct conclusion to the celebration of the Supper is for the community to go out to the sound of instruments making music and voices lifted in song. It may seem like a nice and respectful custom to sit down again at the end of the service and listen attentively to the postlude until it is finished, in order then to exit quietly. But this custom is a sign of a declining liturgical sensibility. A worship service is not a concert. As Volp rightly puts it: "To go out only after all instruments have fallen silent destroys the festive mood. . . . The cry *Ite missa est* ('Go, you are dismissed') from the first centuries recalls the profane call to connect a festive mood and the act of departing. A concluding procession can most clearly express this mutual act of blessing and departing."[2]

Joy, a festive mood, a grateful glorification of God that extends even beyond thanksgiving for the gifts of creation, joy in the presence of Christ that now stands in the light of his resurrection and exaltation, a grateful acceptance of the powers of the Holy Spirit, which enable creatures to resist the powers of sin and death, and in all these things the joy of receiving a share in God's good power, of having been strengthened with the bread and wine from heaven — all this is included in the peace with which human beings go from the Supper into the everyday world.

Results

In connection with the thanksgiving to the Creator, the greeting of peace witnesses to our readiness to join in God's action toward us. Bread and wine as gifts of creation are expressions of peace. Similarly, with the greeting "God's peace be with you" and the response "And also with you," those who celebrate the Supper can give symbolic expression to this peace of creation in relations between human beings.

In the context of the remembrance of Christ, the *anamnesis,* the community asks for Christ's peace: a peace that the community cannot manufacture; a peace that, in view of the cross and of the world's sin, can only be a gift; a peace for which the community can only pray: "Christ, lamb of God, give us your peace."

In connection with the invocation of the Holy Spirit *(epiklesis),* the experience of the gift of divine peace becomes an experience of great joy. Human beings receive a share in the divine powers. They are deemed worthy of being bearers of God's presence on this earth. Through the gifts of the new creation, they are given a share in eternal life, in the divine life. The celebration of the Supper appropriately concludes with a mood of joy and festivity. Strengthened, comforted, encouraged, and raised up by the Supper, human beings go into the everyday world, set free and happy.

2. Rainer Volp, *Liturgik: Die Kunst, Gott zu feiern,* vol. 2, *Theorien und Gestaltung* (Gütersloh: Gütersloher, 1994), p. 1213. Adolf Adam, *The Eucharistic Celebration: The Source and Summit of Faith* (Collegeville, Minn.: Liturgical Press, 1994), pp. 120ff., emphasizes that "Go in peace" expresses the substance of *Ite missa est.*

CHAPTER 12

"In the Name of God, the Father and the Son and the Holy Spirit"

The Presence and Activity of the Triune God in the Supper as Source of Spiritual Renewal

What happens in holy communion? The twelfth answer is: *In the celebration of holy communion human beings enter into a relationship with the triune God. They encounter the living God, the Creator who created them and preserves their life, who is revealed in Jesus Christ as the liberator from the power of sin, and who as Holy Spirit raises human beings up and enables them to be bearers of God's faithful, liberating, and life-giving presence.*

From Concentration on Jesus Christ to Concentration on the Living Triune God

Under the pressure to accommodate to modern thought, the Christian faith has in many parts of the world become banal and devoid of substance. The abstract certainty of a "relation of dependence," a "relation of origin," or an internal relation to a "wholly other" assumed the place of a lively, articulate faith in the living God. But when God is nothing more than an "ultimate point of reference," human beings become indifferent to this "God." And when theology and church talk about God in a way that neglects the linguistic and imaginal world of faith, and instead continually propagate empty and abstract notions of God, the need for spirituality and for solid spiritual footing seeks out other sources and other dialogue partners.

In the midst of the massive "self-secularization" (Wolfgang Huber) of Christian churches, and in the midst of the Christian faith's becoming banal and devoid of content — a process to which, at least in the Western industrialized nations, theologies and churches have themselves made a major contribution — the ecumenical agreement in the twentieth century concerning the Supper has opened new perspectives. The shared efforts to clarify what happens in holy communion have opened up new ways of access to faith in the living God, who for Christian faith is the *triune God.* Already in 1976 Anglicans and Orthodox were saying: "The Eucharist is the action of the Holy Trinity."[1] The 1988 "Meissen Statement" of Anglicans and the German Evangelical church explicitly says: "We believe that the church of the triune God is founded and will be preserved by God's saving action in word and sacrament."[2] The ecumenical documents elaborate with increasing clarity the conviction that we must perceive in the Supper the activity of the triune God, and in this activity, God's vitality and favor toward human beings.

The intra-Protestant conversations concerning the Supper persisted into the 1980s in emphasizing that the entire event of holy communion is to be concentrated on Jesus Christ and his presence (see especially chapter 5). The interconfessional conversations with non-Reformation churches picked up this christological and christocentric emphasis, but expanded it in terms of trinitarian theology.

In this process, Orthodox theology exercised a sizable influence. Orthodox theology has always emphasized that human beings celebrating the Supper are drawn into Christ's presence by *God's Spirit.* Only through the activity of the Holy Spirit does Christ become present in the Supper. Even the Lutheran-Reformed conversations had made cautious moves in the direction of a *trinitarian* understanding of the Supper when, for instance, they spoke of the thanksgiving to the Father, or reflected upon the relation of word and Spirit. Yet these remained only hints that still needed to be developed into trinitarian theological perspectives.

New ground for the trinitarian understanding of the Supper was broken by a dialogue in France, "the group of Les Dombes, which had existed since 1937, and which was composed of Catholic, Lutheran, and Reformed theologians, but which had no official status. In 1972 it presented a text under the title 'On the Way to One and the Same Faith,'"

1. "Moscow Statement" 1976 [A-RC], p. 46.

2. *On the Way to Visible Unity,* pp. 7, 16.

and participated in an exchange with the Commission for Faith and Order of the World Council of Churches, which in 1971 published the study "The Eucharist in Ecumenical Thought."[3] As Lessing correctly highlights, both texts offer at heart a trinitarian structure, inasmuch as they consider the Supper in the perspectives of thanksgiving to the Father, remembrance (*anamnesis*/memorial) of Christ, and gift of the Holy Spirit. In doing so they provide a model for many further studies, among them the important Lutheran–Roman Catholic text "The Eucharist" (1978), and above all "Baptism, Eucharist and Ministry,"[4] which admittedly speaks of the invocation *(epiklesis)* of the Spirit rather than the gift of the Holy Spirit.

Thanksgiving to the God of Creation, Preservation, and New Creation

In holy communion we thank and praise God the Creator in manifold ways. In doing so we have various experiences of God the Creator. We grow in our familiarity with God and God's activity. We thank God not only for bread and wine as gifts of creation. We thank God not only as human beings thank God before a meal. The thanksgiving is more comprehensive. In the Supper we thank the Creator not only for nourishment that satisfies the body. Beyond physical satisfaction, we center on the significance of the "gifts of creation," the elements. The gifts of creation are real signs of peace and of beneficent order. Human beings and other creatures, nature and culture must creatively collaborate in order for bread and wine to come to the table, and specifically to the Lord's table. By God's creative power and through the divine Spirit, God makes possible this creative collaboration. This is reason for great thanks. But above and beyond bread and wine as

3. Eckhard Lessing, *Abendmahl,* Bensheimer Ökumenische Studienhefte 1 (Göttingen: Vandenhoeck, 1993), p. 44, cf. pp. 44-45; "Auf dem Wege zu ein und demselben Glauben?" in G. Gassmann and M. Lienhard et al., eds., *Um Amt und Herrenmahl: Dokumente zum evangelisch/römisch-katholischen Gespräch,* 2nd ed. (Frankfurt, 1974), pp. 104-12; "The Eucharist in Ecumenical Thought," in *Louvain 1971: Study Reports and Documents,* Faith and Order Paper 59 (Geneva: WCC), pp. 71-77.

4. See Lessing, *Abendmahl,* p. 45. John Reumann, *The Supper of the Lord: The New Testament, Ecumenical Dialogues, and Faith and Order on Eucharist* (Philadelphia: Fortress, 1985), pp. 149ff., presents a subtle comparison of the trinitarian structuring of the ecumenical pronouncements.

signs of God's creative and preserving activity, we also recognize other signs of peace in the celebration of the Supper, which are not things that go without saying. The fact that many people gather healthily, festively, and peacefully; the fact that God's word is proclaimed to them; the fact that they can sing and pray in concert; the fact that they can accept one another and listen to one another; the fact that they can jointly upbuild each other; the fact that they can rejoice together — these and many other things are reasons to praise and to thank God the Creator.

Even in times and circumstances that are difficult personally, economically, politically, or in other regards, the celebration of the Supper is the place to thank God for the fact that the world is continually being preserved from chaos, that over and over again, seed time and harvest are possible, and that over and over again, joy and peace are spread among human beings. In times and life situations that are good, the Supper is a high point in the glorification of God: "Praise to the Lord, who o'er all things is wondrously reigning!" In bad times it is the light of hope. At the least, we taste and see, here and now, "that the Lord is good." It is reason to ask God for the clearer activity of the Spirit, for the bestowal of peace — outside of the meal celebration, too — and for the fulfillment of the divine promises.

In holy communion we encounter God not only as the Creator and preserver of the world, but also as the God of salvation and new creation. The living God is self-revealing not only as the Creator. God is self-revealing in clarity in the crucified and risen Jesus Christ. And God is self-revealing in the Holy Spirit, who acts toward, in, and among us human beings. When we recognize, through the revelation of the triune God, the Creator's work of deliverance and new creation, we are, as it were, swept along beyond thanks and praise to the glorification of God, to *doxology.* We recognize in the gifts of bread and wine not only gifts of creation, but gifts of the new creation. We see in the daily food and in the festive drink not only means of life, given to us by the Creator, but gifts that permit us a share in God's eternal life.

The Memory of the Saving, Crucified, Resurrected, and Coming Jesus Christ

It continues to be very difficult for many people to recognize and worship God in Jesus Christ. They equate Jesus Christ with the pre-Easter Jesus, because for them the reality of the risen Christ is unimaginable. The christological concentration in the context of the Supper will not remove this difficulty with one fell swoop. But it can be a decisive aid in growing into belief in the divinity of Christ, and into the recognition that in him we encounter "God from God, light from light, true God from true God." Just as in the Supper we have various experiences of God the Creator and grow in familiarity with God and God's activity, so we also have various experiences of the crucified and risen Christ, which make us more familiar with him.

In this connection we must not understand the "memory of Christ" as a mere recollection of him. To be sure, recollection of the pre-Easter Jesus is of central importance. It permeates and shapes all our relations to the presence of the risen, exalted, and "coming" Lord. But the Risen One is with us, around us, and in us by his Spirit. The risen Christ brings us together. We call ourselves "Christians" after him. We celebrate the Supper after his example and in response to his command. In the Supper, the risen and exalted Christ is present not only as the recollected Jesus. His body and blood are sensuously present in the gifts of creation and new creation, in bread and wine. They are present in the bread and the wine, over which God has been thanked "in remembrance of Christ," and which are given and taken, taken and given, eaten and drunk "in remembrance of Christ." Christ's body and blood are present in the "elements" of the Supper — not in just any piece of bread or just any sip of wine.

In order to understand this presence, we must understand the meaning of the celebration of the Supper and of "memory of Christ." We must see that it is in the "night of betrayal" that Jesus institutes the Supper and promises his bodily presence in bread and wine. He promises his presence in the jeopardization of human beings' communion with him, with God, and with each other. Yet holy communion focuses not only on threats and dangers, but on the actual catastrophe, the actual attempt of human beings to destroy their relationship with God. The death of Christ is proclaimed. The night of God-forsakenness; hell on earth; the recognition that religion, law (Jewish and Roman!), politics, morality, and public opinion are misused; the recognition that even friendship and discipleship are not dependable — all this belongs to the "memory of Christ." The Supper confronts us with God's gifts of creation and the human destruction of relationship to God, with God's peace and human violence, with God's goodness and human rejection of what is good. The Supper confronts us with all that, and not just peripherally, but at the very center.

We see the torn body and the shed blood in the good gifts of creation. The Risen One is present to us as the Crucified One. As often as we eat this bread and drink the cup, we proclaim the Lord's death!

But inasmuch as the crucified Christ is present to our senses in the bread and wine of holy communion, he is present to us as comforter and savior. He is present to us as the one who establishes reconciliation with God and reconciliation between human beings. He is present as the power of this reconciliation. Glory to God in the highest and peace on earth are symbolically realized in the Supper. Human beings are delivered from the chaos of the cross, from the night of God-forsakenness, and from the triumph of sin and death. They are given the capacity for new communion with God and with each other. God does not abandon them to this destructive power and their lovelessness. Through Christ's activity and in Christ, God saves and renews human beings and God's endangered creation. The "memory of Christ" — which recollects both the fundamental jeopardization of creation by the power of sin and God's saving action, which proclaims and symbolically demonstrates both danger and deliverance — this memory of Christ is filled with Christ's presence (see chapter 8). In this memory, the whole Christ comes into play, with all the dimensions and facets of his activity. The entire fullness of Christ's life is active in this memory. This memory is creative not only in making Christ present. It engages in creation and new creation inasmuch as human beings who bear witness to Christ are shaped and transformed by this memory. By growing in their relationship to God and to Christ, by blossoming in their own persons and strengthening one another, human beings are transformed. They are renewed and raised up by the Spirit of Christ.

Invocation of the Enlivening, Liberating, and Uplifting Holy Spirit

If we want to get clear about God's presence and activity among human beings, we must talk about God's Spirit. Through the Holy Spirit, God works among creatures. Through the Holy Spirit they are connected, strengthened, preserved, and renewed. Through the Spirit they are brought into communion with the risen Christ. In the Spirit the risen Christ is near them and active among them. Through the Spirit they are enabled to act in remembrance of him and to live in this memory. The activity of the Holy Spirit in the Supper is source and leaven: for the creation of community both between human beings and God, and among human beings; for the reestablishment of justice; and for the liberation of human beings from the power of sin.

Many people — especially in the classical churches of the Western industrialized nations — have difficulty with the experience of the Holy Spirit.[5] They have a hard time recognizing God in the Holy Spirit. In the celebration of holy communion, familiarity with the Holy Spirit can grow because here, too, we can have various experiences of the God who surrounds us "from every side," and who works in and among us. The Holy Spirit gathers and concentrates the church of Christ in the Supper. The Spirit gathers concrete communities, but also places them in the broad context of the church of all times and regions of the world. The Holy Spirit is God's power of creative engagement with chaos and sin — a power in which no less and none other than God is present. In the Holy Spirit God is present in a different manner than as Creator and in Jesus Christ. At the same time, the Holy Spirit is so intimately connected with the Creator and with Jesus Christ that we can speak of the Creator-Spirit and of the Spirit of Christ. Through the Creator and in the Spirit, creatures are preserved in the peace of creation. Through Jesus Christ and the Spirit, they are rescued from jeopardization and self-jeopardization under the power of sin. Through the activity of the triune God in the Spirit, they are given powers that enable them to resist the might of sin. They are given powers to accept God's renewal of the relationship with human beings, and accordingly to renew relations between human beings. The Spirit turns violent humans into peaceful beings. The Spirit takes loveless creatures whose relationship to love is one of pure need, and turns them into loving human beings, themselves worthy of love.

In the Spirit, God's faithfulness to community embraces human beings. To express this, theology has chosen the difficult term "justification." God gives human beings faith, in which they — both individually and communally — enter into relationship with God, and in which they can live in this relationship, in God's faithfulness to community. God gives human beings the "memory of Christ," which they are permitted to preserve, cultivate, and spread in proclamation, in love, in compassion, in the readiness to forgive one another, and also in the celebration of holy communion. Receiving these powers, human beings are bound into

5. Cf. M. Welker, *God the Spirit,* trans. John F. Hoffmeyer (Minneapolis: Fortress, 1994), pp. 1ff.

God's life. They become "new creatures," members of the body of Christ. They receive a tremendous worth. They are enabled to be nothing less than bearers of God's presence. For this, theology has used the term *sanctification.* When God's Spirit sanctifies human beings, the Spirit raises them up, gives them a share in a life that can no longer be destroyed. They receive a share in the life of the risen Christ. They receive a share in eternal life.

The Eternal Riches of God in the Poverty of the Supper

The trinitarian perspectives opened by the Supper intersect and engage each other in manifold ways. They permeate each other, just as the living God's three modes of being permeate each other *(perichoresis).* The threatened and good creation, the might of sin and the power of deliverance, the jeopardization of communion both with God and among each other, and the power of temporal and eternal life — in the celebration of the Supper, all this is present and interconnected in a way cogently and clearly narrated and understood. The Lutherans and Roman Catholics have tied this trinitarian orientation to the christological concentration:

> Finally, the mystery of the Eucharist unites us to the ultimate mystery from, through, and towards which all things exist: the mystery of the triune God. Our heavenly Father is the first source and final goal of the eucharistic event. The incarnate Son of God is the living centre of the eucharistic event: the one in, with and through whom it unfolds. The Holy Spirit is the immeasurable power of love which gives the Eucharist life and lasting effect. . . . This most profound mystery of the Lord's Supper and of our life is celebrated at the end of many eucharistic prayers in the doxology. In view of the presence of our Lord Jesus Christ, it says: "Through him, with him, in him/in the unity of the Holy Spirit/all honour and glory is yours, almighty Father/now and forever. Amen."[6]

6. "The Eucharist" 1978 [L-RC], pp. 194-95. Cf. "Baptism, Eucharist and Ministry" 1982 [WCC], p. 478; "The Mystery of the Church" 1982 [O-RC], p. 55. Concerning the relation between sacramental theology and "trinitarian Christology," see Louis-Marie Chauvet, *Symbole et sacrament: Une relecture sacramentelle de l'existence chrétienne* (Paris: Cerf, 1987), pp. 459ff.

In glorifying God and in glorifying Christ we make clear that the difference between God and human beings, between Creator and creatures is not abolished by the experience that the renewed creation is set free and raised up, and that great worth is thereby conferred upon it. In petition, thanksgiving, and glorification, human beings celebrating the Supper recognize that they are dependent upon God's work of creation and new creation. In invoking the Spirit they know that even when they are filled with the Spirit, when they are being built up into the body of Christ, when they are given faith, love, and hope and many gifts of the Spirit *(charismata),* they cannot exhaust God's power or lay exclusive claim to it. By perceiving with their own senses the risen and exalted Christ in the bread and wine of the Supper, they are conscious that they are fundamentally dependent upon God. Indeed they are conscious of the poverty and pitiableness of earthly existence before God.

In the Supper, this consciousness of poverty and pitiableness becomes clear in manifold ways: The action is merely symbolic; the knowledge of salvation remains jeopardized; the memory of betrayal and crucifixion is renewed; the knowledge of resurrection remains controverted; the "heavenly eucharist" still lies in the distance; it is hard to imagine the ecumenical church of all times and regions of the world in the often small community, beset with troubles. In the celebration of the Supper, the church knows that it is still underway. It knows that the universally evident presence of Christ, his *parousia* "in glory," is still outstanding. Precisely the sensuous experience of the presence of Christ in bread and wine is a great cause for humility. Precisely the sensuous concentration on bread and wine and on the symbolic action of the Supper makes clear: Here we are still standing at the beginning of a journey. To be sure, here we are standing in the most intimate conceivable relationship with God. Here we can experience God with our senses, in a bodily manner. To be sure, here we are standing in genuine, unobscured human community. Here "peace on earth among those whom God favors" is indeed occurring — however transitory and fragile that occurrence might be. But in all this, human beings in holy communion stand again and again at the beginning of a journey. They stand at a beginning that invites them, from their poverty and lostness, continually to accept anew God's favor and to set out toward God.

Results

At the end of the twentieth century, the ecumenical conversations of the churches concerning the Supper have led to a strong concentration on the working of the triune God in the Supper. Many documents of ecumenical understanding have accepted the structure: thanksgiving to the Creator (eucharist), remembrance of Christ (memorial, *anamnesis*), and invocation of the Holy Spirit *(epiklesis)*.

The recognition of God's work of creation and new creation in holy communion can contribute to a renewal of faith and of spirituality, which many persons today are seeking. Ideas of God emptied of content, which do not provide people with secure footing and which have condemned the faith to silence, can be replaced by a new process of becoming familiar with God and God's presence. God's vitality and love can be recognized in the Trinity's work of creating, delivering, and raising up creatures. In the celebration of the Supper, we encounter the rich work of the triune God woven together in a way that can be cogently and clearly narrated and understood. In the poverty of a symbolic meal, God grants the divine glory to human beings.

APPENDIX

Documents of the "Growth in Agreement" of Churches on the Global Level in Questions of Holy Communion, in Chronological Order, 1931-1990

To make it easier for readers to find their way, the specific churches, confessions, organizations, or religious movements involved in each particular document are designated in brackets, unless the participants are named explicitly in the document's title. A large number of the documents listed below are cited from one of the following collections:

1. Harding Meyer and Lukas Vischer, eds., *Growth in Agreement: Reports and Agreed Statements of Ecumenical Conversations on a World Level*, Ecumenical Documents II, Faith and Order Paper 108 (New York: Paulist Press, 1984).
2. John Borelli and John H. Erickson, eds., *The Quest for Unity: Orthodox and Catholics in Dialogue: Documents of the Joint International Commission and Official Dialogues in the United States, 1965-1995* (Crestwood, N.Y.: St. Vladimir's Seminary Press; Washington, D.C.: United States Catholic Conference, 1996).
3. William G. Rusch and Jeffrey Gros, eds., *Deepening Communion: International Ecumenical Documents with Roman Catholic Participation* (Washington, D.C.: United States Catholic Conference, 1998).

A = Anglican
B = Baptist
CB = Czech Brethren
D = Disciples of Christ
E = Evangelical
L = Lutheran
M = Methodist
O = Orthodox
OC = Old Catholic
P = Pentecostal
R = Reformed
RC = Roman Catholic
SO = Syrian Orthodox
U = Union (of Lutheran and Reformed in Europe)
W = Waldensian
WCC = World Council of Churches

For example: Denver Report 1971 [M-RC], *Growth in Agreement,* pp. 308-39, esp. pp. 325-31; cited as "Denver Report." This means that in 1971 a document was published issuing from a conversation between Methodists and Roman Catholics. The text is published in *Growth in Agreement* on pp. 308-39. The statements that are important for the understanding of the Supper are found primarily on pp. 325-31.

If the original language of publication was other than English, the citation for that language is appended to the English citation.

1931 Bonn Agreement [A-OC], *Growth in Agreement,* pp. 37-38.

1937 Declaration of the Second Session of the Fourth Confessing Synod of the Evangelical Church of the Old Prussian Union in Halle [L-R], in Gerhard Niemöller, ed., *Die Synode zu Halle 1937: Die zweite Tagung der vierten Bekenntnissynode der Evangelischen Kirche der altpreupischen Union: Text — Dokumente — Berichte* (Göttingen, 1963); cited as Niemöller, *Synode zu Halle.*

1957-62 Arnoldshain Theses on the Supper, with Clarifications [L-R], *Das Mahl des Herrn: 25 Jahre nach Arnoldshain: Ein Votum des theologischen Ausschusses der Arnoldshainer Konferenz* (Neukirchen-Vluyn: Neukirchener, 1982); cited as *Arnoldshain.*

1966 Joint Worship at Ecumenical Gatherings [WCC-RC], *Work Book for the Assembly Committees, Prepared for the Fourth Assembly of the World Council of Churches* (Geneva: World Council of Churches, 1968), pp. 115-17.

1971 Eucharistic Doctrine (Windsor Statement) [A-RC], *Growth in Agreement,* pp. 68-72; cited as "Windsor Statement."

1971 Denver Report [M-RC], *Growth in Agreement,* pp. 308-39, esp. pp. 325-31; cited as "Denver Report."

1972 Pullach Report [A-L], *Growth in Agreement,* pp. 14-33, esp. pp. 22-31; cited as "Pullach Report."

1972 Malta Report [L-RC], *Growth in Agreement,* pp. 168-89, esp. pp. 184-88; cited as "Malta Report."

1973 Agreement between the Reformation Churches of Europe (Leuenberg Agreement) [CB-L-R-U-W], *The Leuenberg Agreement and Lutheran-Reformed Relationships: Evaluations by North American and European Theologians* (Minneapolis: Augsburg, 1989), pp. 144-54, esp. pp. 147-49; cited as *Leuenberg.*

1973 Ministry and Ordination (Canterbury Statement) [A-RC], *Growth in Agreement,* pp. 78-84; cited as "Ministry and Ordination."

1976 Moscow Statement [A-O], *Growth in Agreement,* pp. 41-49, esp. pp. 45-46; cited as "Moscow Statement."

1976 Dublin Report [M-RC], *Growth in Agreement,* pp. 340-66, esp. pp. 351-61; cited as "Dublin Report."

1977 The Presence of Christ in Church and World [R-RC], *Growth in Agreement,* pp. 434-63, esp. pp. 449-61; cited as "The Presence of Christ."

1978 The Eucharist [L-RC], *Growth in Agreement,* pp. 190-214; cited as "The Eucharist."

1979 The Unity of the Church and the Local Churches (Bonn Agreed Statement) [O-OC], *Growth in Agreement,* pp. 404-6; cited as "The Unity of the Church." Original German: "Die Einheit der Kirche und die Ortskirchen," in Harding Meyer et al., eds., *Dokumente wachsender Übereinstimmung: Sämtliche Berichte und Konsenstexte interkonfessioneller Gespräche auf Weltebene,* vol. 1 (Paderborn: Bonifatius; Frankfurt: Otto Lembeck, 1983), pp. 40-41.

1979 Eucharistic Doctrine: Elucidation [A-RC], *Growth in Agreement,* pp. 72-77; cited as "Eucharistic Doctrine: Elucidation."

1980 Ways to Community [L-RC], *Growth in Agreement,* pp. 214-40, esp. pp. 228-33; cited as "Ways to Community."

1981 Final Report [A-RC], *Growth in Agreement,* pp. 62-67, esp. pp. 65-67; cited as "Final Report."

1981 The Ministry in the Church [L-RC], *Growth in Agreement,* pp. 248-75, esp. pp. 256-58.

1982 Lima Report: Baptism, Eucharist and Ministry [WCC], *Growth in Agreement,* pp. 466-503, esp. pp. 475-82; cited as "Baptism, Eucharist and Ministry."

1982 The Mystery of the Church and of the Eucharist in the Light of the Mystery of the Holy Trinity [O-RC], *Quest for Unity,* pp. 53-64; cited as "The Mystery of the Church." Original French in *Episkepsis* 277 (1982).

1982 Final Report of the Dialogue Between the Secretariat for Promoting Christian Unity of the Roman Catholic Church and Some Classical Pentecostals (1977-1982) [P-RC], *Deepening Communion,* pp. 379-97, esp. pp. 386-87.

1983 "Joint Statement of the Orthodox–Old Catholic Theological Commission" (Chambésy Statement), Urs von Arx, ed., *Koinonia auf altkirchlicher Basis: Beiheft zur Internationalen Kirchlichen Zeitschrift* 79 (1989): 76-77; cited as "Chambésy Statement."

1983 *Anglican-Lutheran Dialogue: The Report of the European Commission* (London: SPCK, 1983), esp. pp. 11-12.

1984 *Anglican-Orthodox Dialogue: The Dublin Agreed Statement 1984* (Crestwood, N.Y.: St. Vladimir's Seminary Press, 1985); cited as *Dublin Statement,* esp. pp. 14-15 and 47.

1984 *God's Reign and Our Unity: The Report of the Anglican-Reformed International Commission 1981-1984* (London: SPCK; Edinburgh: The Saint Andrew Press, 1984), esp. pp. 39-45.

1984 *Lutheran-Methodist Dialogue, 1979-1984: The Church: Community of Grace* (Geneva: Lutheran World Federation; Lake Junaluska: World Methodist Council, 1984).

1984 The Evangelical–Roman Catholic Dialogue on Mission [E-RC], *Deepening Communion,* pp. 427-78, esp. pp. 457-58; cited as "Dialogue on Mission."

1984 Facing Unity: Models, Forms, and Phases of Catholic-Lutheran Church Fellowship [L-RC], *Deepening Communion,* pp. 15-71, esp. pp. 17-49; cited as "Facing Unity."

1984 Statement of Pope John Paul II and the Syrian-Orthodox Patriarch of Antioch and the Entire East, Ignatius Zacca I. Ivas, on Mutual Pastoral Aid 1984 [RC-SO]; cited as "Mutual Pastoral Aid."

1985 Joint Statement of the Orthodox–Old Catholic Theological Commission (Amersfoort Statement), Urs von Arx, ed., *Koinonia auf altkirchlicher Basis: Beiheft zur Internationalen Kirchlichen Zeitschrift* 79 (1989): 210ff.; cited as "Amersfoort Statement."

1987 *The Niagara Report: Report of the Anglican-Lutheran Consultation on Episcope 1987* (London: Anglican Consultative Council; Geneva: Lutheran World Federation, 1988), esp. pp. 34-39; cited as *Niagara Report.*

1987 *Towards Closer Fellowship: Report of the Dialogue between Reformed and Disciples of Christ,* Studies from the World Alliance of Reformed

Churches 11 (Geneva: WARC, 1988), esp. pp. 8-9; cited as *Towards Closer Fellowship.*

1987 Faith, Sacraments and the Unity of the Church [O-RC], *Quest for Unity,* pp. 93-104. Original French in *Episkepsis* 390.

1988 The Sacrament of Order in the Sacramental Structure of the Church with Particular Reference to the Importance of Apostolic Succession for the Sanctification and Unity of the People of God [O-RC], *Quest for Unity,* pp. 131-42, esp. pp. 134-39.

1988 *On the Way to Visible Unity: A Joint Statement of the Church of England, the Federation of the Evangelical Churches in the German Democratic Republic, and the Evangelical Church of Germany* (Meissen Statement) [A-L-R] (Berlin and Hannover: 1988); cited as *On the Way to Visible Unity.*

1989 Perspectives on *Koinonia* [P-RC], *Deepening Communion,* pp. 399-422, esp. pp. 414-17; cited as "Perspectives on *Koinonia.*"

1990 *Baptists and Lutherans in Conversation: A Message to Our Churches: Report of the Joint Commission of the Baptist World Alliance and the Lutheran World Federation* (Geneva: Baptist World Alliance, 1990), esp. pp. 35-36; cited as *A Message to Our Churches.*

1990 *Toward Church Fellowship: Report of the Joint Commission of the Lutheran World Federation and the World Alliance of Reformed Churches* (Geneva: LWF, 1989), esp. pp. 11-27; cited as *Toward Church Fellowship.*

1990 Towards a Common Understanding of the Church [R-RC], *Deepening Communion,* pp. 179-229, esp. pp. 218-25; cited as "Towards a Common Understanding."

Epilogue and Acknowledgments

This book is a product of courses in Heidelberg and Princeton, especially a lecture course offered during the 1994/95 winter semester at the University of Heidelberg and lectures held at Princeton Theological Seminary at the end of 1995. I am grateful to many of the auditors of those lectures for their critical and clarifying questions and comments, especially Dr. Sigrid Brandt, Dr. Ernst Schnellbächer, and a group of women students at Princeton who, among other things, caused me to form a new judgment about the question of the "admission" of children to the Supper. I am grateful to Mr. Gregory Faulkner for helpful bibliographic suggestions concerning Orthodox theology, especially the theology of Alexander Schmemann.

When I was working on a lecture on "The Resurrection" for the 1993 Frederick Neumann Symposium on the Theological Interpretation of Scripture at Princeton Theological Seminary,[1] I gained a new perspective that has had major consequences for the way I have chosen here to handle the theme of "holy communion." I am indebted to my colleagues Daniel Migliore and Klaus Berger for their good critical reflections on that lecture. I received further helpful insights from an advanced seminar in sacramental theology in the 1994 summer semester at Heidelberg. I am

1. M. Welker, "Resurrection and the Reign of God," in Daniel Migliore, ed., *The Princeton Seminary Bulletin,* Supplementary Issue 3: *The 1993 Frederick Neumann Symposium on the Theological Interpretation of Scripture: Hope for the Kingdom and Responsibility for the World* (Princeton, 1994).

thankful to the doctoral candidates and other students who participated in this seminar for their fruitful discussion of classical and contemporary positions in sacramental theology. In particular, I have learned much from Dr. Günter Thomas and Dr. Andreas Schüle. I am grateful to Mr. Johannes Wachowski for bibliographic references concerning Jewish festival culture.

I would like gratefully to highlight a particularly valuable basis for my investigations: Eckhard Lessing's book *Abendmahl,* Bensheimer Ökumenische Studienhefte 1 (Göttingen: Vandenhoeck, 1993).

Finally, I thank the colleagues of the "Pfullingen workgroup" and the students of the Pfullingen graduate collegium for their constructive engagement with my sketch on the theme "Church and Supper," from which my work on this book also profited.[2]

With the eyes of an expert in German language and literature, with common sense, and with a sensitivity to the shape and flow of theological reflection, my wife Ulrike Welker has read, criticized, and improved the text. I am grateful to her not only for her collaboration on this book, but also for the continual, always stimulating and instructive conversation concerning foundations and limit questions of faith.

I cordially thank Dr. John Hoffmeyer for the translation.

Michael Welker
Heidelberg, Summer 1999

2. M. Welker, "Kirche und Abendmahl," in Wilfried Härle and Reiner Preul, eds., *Kirche: Marburger Jahrbuch Theologie VIII* (Marburg: Elwert Verlag, 1996), pp. 47-60.

Index of Subjects and Names

Index of Scripture References